voices

in the

hills

Collected Ramblings
from a Rural Life

NESSA FLAX

BUNKER HILL
PUBLISHING

These mountains know more than they tell,
yes, and more than you or I ever will.
There's magic hiding underneath a country windowsill,
and there're voices in the hills.

—Dick McCormack, singer, songwriter,
and Vermont state senator

This book is dedicated to small-town
newspapers everywhere . . .

to the people who work to keep them alive

the businesses that advertise in them

the people who read them—

And especially to the *Journal Opinion*'s
publisher emeritus Robert Huminski

and current publisher Connie Sanville,

thank you.

www.bunkerhillpublishing.com
by Bunker Hill Publishing Inc.
285 River Road, Piermont
New Hampshire 03779, USA

10 9 8 7 6 5 4 3 2 1

"Voices in the Hills" and "Rare Ones and Fair Ones" song
lyrics used with permission, copyright Dick McCormack.

Library of Congress Control Number: 2012930407

ISBN 978-1-59373-095-6

Designed by Joe Lops
Printed in Canada

contents

foreword

by Cicely Richardson

When I joined the *Journal Opinion* in 1996, I inherited the duty of editing Nessa Flax's weekly column, "Rambling Reflections." Years ago, these reflections found their home on page four of the *Journal Opinion*, beneath the editorial (except when bumped slightly to the side by an extrawordy editor).

An independent, locally owned weekly newspaper, the *JO* covers more than a dozen small Vermont and New Hampshire towns, with populations from six hundred to forty-seven hundred, spanning the Connecticut River.

Editing with Nessa was always an adventure. Nearly every week for the ten years I was managing editor of the *JO*, we'd roll up our sleeves and tackle her column together in our quest for the best way to convey her thoughts and observations. Occasionally in person and more often by phone, we wrestled over words, phrases, and those pernicious dangling participles.

In her ramblings, Nessa captures the place, the people, and her connections with her adopted North Country home—reflecting the light, colors, and moods of the seasons, reflecting on friends and neighbors, their habits, and the lessons she learns from them.

Some rambles become rants on the vicissitudes of life and change. Others convey Nessa's quirky, philosophical, or delightfully witty reflections on the wider world. New experiences rekindle childhood memories of her grandmother's garden, her father's infectious love of football, her mother's knack for choosing perfect peaches.

Local readers and distant subscribers know where to find "Rambling Reflections." For years, they have clipped favorite columns and asked when Nessa would collect them in a book. Here at last is that book, the product of a lengthy winnowing process over the past several years.

This new task was daunting. We began with more than six hundred columns. Spreading them like decks of cards on a friend's dining room table, we rejected, selected, and culled to narrow them down to the manageable 126 that make up this volume. Then we reedited every one.

Some were clear winners; others were harder to choose. After all, over the years, Nessa has found countless ways to conjure up images of the North Country's amazing autumn glory, its wintry drear, or the bounty and drudgery of a raspberry harvest. How many can you include in one book?

The columns we chose represent the best of "Rambling Reflections," ranging in tone from lighthearted to nostalgic, descriptive to philosophical. They are essentially arranged by seasons within four categories—North Country Life, In the Old House, Transitions, and At Home in the Woods.

Whether you read *Voices in the Hills* from cover to cover, leaf through it for old favorites, or dip into it to ponder a column a night or once a week, I believe you'll come away with new insights or find yourself saying, "I wish I'd written that!"

introduction

After college, I intended to move back to California, where I spent my adolescence and young adulthood.

Nearly forty years later, here I am, still in the North Country. From Hanover, New Hampshire, I followed the Connecticut River north, living for more than a decade in Newbury, Vermont, before settling in Ryegate Corner.

Once, my father teased that I had moved as far away as I could and still be in America. He's not wrong. An easy, under-two-hour drive up Interstate 91 brings me to the Canadian border.

And even all these years later, it's nearly impossible to describe my conversion into a country girl.

Sometimes I say the mountains got into my blood.

Sometimes I think it's the green.

Sometimes I say, hey, if you think it's comforting to go to a bar where everybody knows your name, try living in a cluster of *towns* where that's true.

By the time I began writing my column "Rambling Reflections" for the *Journal Opinion*, I had rambled a bit myself. I worked at a New Hampshire regional magazine, sold motorcycles at a small shop in Vermont—experiencing North Country beauties from the back of friends' bikes, weaving through the landscape on country roads—and had a sixteen-year teaching and coaching career at Oxbow High School in Bradford, Vermont.

There, I was plunged into the complexities of overlapping small-town loyalties, stumbling over historical rivalries and resentments. There, I experienced the joys and sorrows of staying put long enough to watch my students grow up, marry, and, in more cases than my heart could hold, be buried.

Much has been depicted in movies and television or written about rural New Englanders' taciturn natures and disdain for "flatlanders" (referring to outsiders). We have seen them as laughable hicks and narrow-minded hypocrites, as amusing eccentrics and hermits.

The truth is much more complex.

As I suspect is true of most rural areas, life in the North Country is hard. But people here have roots sunk deep into the land and into their small communities. Communities where elected representatives are the folks next door, and campaigns for town offices consist of standing up at town meeting and saying a few words.

My suburban and city background left its mark. The North Country continues to present an ongoing, unfolding introduction into a wholly different way of life.

My columns have chronicled the adventure. Along the way, many native residents of Vermont and New Hampshire have taught me how to live this life with richness and joy.

I hope I have made them proud.

north country life

proprietary pleasures

More than twenty-five years have passed since I moved to the North Country. I find it so strange that I've become old enough to say "a quarter of a century" in reference to a single phase of my life.

Such were my thoughts during a recent meandering drive over back roads with a friend who was raised in this area. Wherever we went, he had a story, a memory woven into the landscape.

A cabin where he'd spent summers as a child. Places where the landscape itself had changed—long-gone swamps now meadow green. Houses where his family had lived, brooks where he had fished.

I recalled a similar drive not long after I came to the North Country. I was with a new friend who'd lived here all his life. I did not understand, then, the proprietary pleasure he took in the land down each dusty road.

But on my recent drive, I had memories, too.

Places I'd lived. Roads where I'd struggled through mud to take students home after school. Grassy plots with new houses where I could remember an old, crumbling barn disassembling itself year by year with odd grace.

As my memories wove themselves through trees and fields, I felt a tug of intertwining bonds . . . the proprietary plea-

sure that once I did not understand. A quiet sort of ownership, though I hold no deeds to the lands where my memories
resonate.

And I remembered a different friend from my early North
Country years. He told me he'd tried to leave several times.
Annually, he talked of moving "before the snow flies." One
night, he laughed and said he was held here by "Vermont's
velvet green chains."

It is a phrase I've never forgotten, and in this rain-washed
verdant spring, I understand it more deeply than ever before.

Somehow, my life has become entwined in the woods. Baptized in the brooks. My footprints are invisibly imprinted along
trails and dirt roads I've walked. Students who once laughed
in my classroom lie in carefully tended cemeteries, lost before
their time. Churches hidden in the hills hosted marriages of
kids who shared their lives with me.

Do we become a part of a place? Or does the place become
a part of us?

Which are the roots, which the branches?

All I know, now, is that it feels like a blessing to be here in
the North Country. A place where I can mark the fall of an
old familiar tree. A place where houses are referred to by the
names of residents who have long passed on but are remembered still.

A place where I note with regret new houses on once-grassy
knolls. Where my mind's eye holds fresh the image of a barn
sinking into the earth, as if going home.

A place I hold in my heart, or that holds me . . . or both.

real vermonters
don't sit down

I spent my early childhood in Virginia. My mother was a gracious lady, blue-blooded in the traditions of Southern hospitality. The rules of Southern culture declare that until a guest sits down and, at the very least, is sipping a cup of something, you've failed to discharge your hallowed duty as a hostess.

A lady's good manners and breeding (as they say in the South) are largely measured by her ability to put guests at ease.

While I lived in California, there was little conflict with these Southern-bred values. There, someone who drops by for a cup of tea might well end up staying until their next life transition.

I didn't realize how thoroughly I'd absorbed my early indoctrination until I moved to the North Country. Here, I consistently failed to get visitors to sit down. Never mind getting them to take a cup of anything.

Half the time, heck, I couldn't even get them to come inside.

How many conversations have you had standing in dooryards, driveways, on front steps, and—the perennial North Country favorite—just inside the kitchen door?

Now, more than twenty years after moving here, I understand that manners and breeding have not failed me.

The truth is, real Vermonters don't sit down.

This strikes me as especially peculiar given our climate. I've held extended conversations standing in the cold drizzle of April rains. I've shivered through interesting chats at eighteen degrees, buffeted by windchill in the single digits. I've listened to Vermont stories while swatting at clouds of blackflies and have been sunburned during dooryard sociability at the height of summer.

I consulted with one of my native Vermont friends about this phenomenon. She offered the explanation that Vermonters have an intense respect for others' privacy. It goes along with their fiercely independent natures.

Vermonters, she said, "don't want to intrude."

Okay. I surrender. Come on over and don't have a cup of tea.

Drop on by, and we'll stand by the door and talk awhile.

woodpile poetry

Stacking wood is an art. A woodpile made by a master has the rhyme and rhythm of a well-crafted poem.

It's true. Ask anyone who remembers what it was like the first time they tried to create a pile from a heap of wood chunks. Ask them what the woodpile looked like. If they're honest, they'll tell tales of leaning, lurching stacks of wood that couldn't be trusted to stay put when left alone.

This is a craft that cannot be taught. I've watched many wood wizards in my time, but I never learned a thing. The best of them seem to just plunk one log atop another. But even in my earliest days of close encounters of the loggy kind, I knew it wasn't that simple. I plunked and my pile hunkered like a malevolent creature, plotting the right moment to turn and dump my laboriously laid logs on my toes.

Over the years, I have no doubt amused and irritated the folks who have delivered and stacked my wood. Because, naturally, I not only watch, I ask questions. Picture that . . .

The average North Country logger simply does not think of himself as a woodpile poet. Ask how he manages to create a perfectly level surface from logs of wildly varying shapes, each with its own eccentricities of knots and knobs and nubs, and he'll pause just long enough to shoot you a look that says that you're one strange duck.

A flatlander for sure.

All this came to mind the other day. I was carrying wood from the shed to the basement and stacking it in front of the furnace. I plunked it down, maybe turned it around, and my stack of wood grew straight and strong, each layer level as a tabletop. Something made me stop and see what I had done.

I just stood there awhile, amazed at the poetry of my pile. Then I laughed out loud. Because I had no idea I'd learned to make rhymes in wood.

Though I know loggers will laugh at me, I think I've stumbled on the secret. If you stop trying to force the wood to stack up the way you want and work with it as it is, the logs find their own way to fit together in harmony, nested knot to knob and nub.

It occurs to me that we'd all get along a whole lot better if we learned from logs and listened to woodpile poetry.

the legacy

Even at eighty he was loose-limbed and lanky, his eyes sparkling with mischief. His jokes were often corny, but he'd tell them with such glee you just had to laugh.

His speech was pure Vermont, which you don't hear much anymore. Deep as the furrows he'd plowed. Smooth as maple syrup, and just as rich. When I listened to him, those amber tones would flow right through me, slowing my breath to the rhythm of the land. Echoes of the seasons' ebb and flow resonated in his voice—the gentle, velvet-steel strength of one who works the earth.

He captained no corporations, funded no foundations, and the world at large never took note of him. But on Monday, August 23, 1999, some two hundred people gathered to celebrate his life, mourn his passing, and lay him to rest.

Al LaBay was an ordinary man. An ordinary man who led an extraordinary life.

It was a life founded on faith, salted with humor, and spiced with joy. In his later years, it was a life decorated with the flowers of his gardens, including his roadside Garden of Weedin' at the heart of Ryegate Corner. He cultivated a bounty of vegetables and raspberries, shared with anyone who knew him. It was the growing he loved, the growing and the giving. He and his wife, Beulah, had modest needs.

You can take the farm from the farmer, but the farmer remains.

Vermont senator and songster Dick McCormack wrote a song memorializing such North Country men:

> *Here's to the rare ones,*
> *here's to the fair ones*
> *who find their way into our lives*
> *to touch them now and then*
> *The gray-haired ones of average size*
> *and what a hurt to realize*
> *when they're gone they'll not be back again;*
> *we may never see their kind again.*

I sat in the church and listened to family and friends speak of Al. I listened as a collective voice was raised in song. I watched as, almost visibly, the community began to work new threads into the tapestry of its life, weaving strands of fond memories and love abiding into the rend left by Al's absence.

This, and more. In celebrating Al's life, we honored the values he lived by. Steward of the land, active citizen, good neighbor, a life of faith practiced—not preached. In this honoring, we reaffirmed the importance of these qualities. I believe this tribute sent each of us home with renewed inspiration to transcend the press of busy-ness and reach out, with joy, to others.

As I looked around at the men, women and children who gathered in remembrance, comforted by bread (and brownies) broken in fellowship, I thought that perhaps my songwriting friend is wrong.

. . . Perhaps the rare and fair ones leave a legacy that burns so bright, others are forged in the light of their lives.

front-door phenomenon

Quick—how many people do you know actually use their front doors? Special occasions don't count.

When I first moved here, I drove around quite a bit to get to know the area. I couldn't figure out why so many homes that otherwise appeared to be finished had no steps leading to the front door. I saw trailers with front doors dangling, houses with front doors hovering.

Now I understand. When you're building or renovating, money's tight. You spend it on necessities first. Plumbing, electricity, blasting through ledge to put in a septic system—all these essentials gobble up bucks quicker than folks at a wild game supper. But the ability to use your front door? That's a frill.

I suspect the problem is that most homes aren't designed for rough North Country living.

Take our front door. It opens into a small space at the base of the main stairs to the second floor. With the front door open, say "Mother-may-I?" and it's only one giant step forward to stair one. For me, that is, and I'm only five foot two. For Neil, it's a baby step.

Everyone with equally ill-planned front doors, raise your hands.

We have another entry through the enclosed front porch and into the kitchen. This door makes sense. Plenty of room for depositing muddy shoes, kicking the snow off your boots, wiping dog paws, and setting down groceries out of the rain, as well as a protected place for the UPS man to leave packages.

I have friends with so-called second entryways into mudrooms as cluttered as hall closets. Wonderful places. A mudroom tells the family's story in boots, jackets, shirts, gloves, and hats. Hobbies and habits are revealed in haberdashery hanging on public display.

While pondering this curious state of construction, I asked a local contractor if he'd noticed this front-door phenomenon. North Country carpenters are not accustomed to such queries, so at first Ted looked at me oddly. But then he said I had a point.

"Why have a front door at all?" I asked. "And if you already have one, why not seal it up tight and leave it be?"

"Habit?" he proposed.

That's my guess. A house without a front door would just seem incomplete, awkward, deprived.

So the next time you hear a nasty crack about how tight Yankee Northerners are, just remember: We're the folks who indulge in the fanciful frivolity of front doors we hardly ever, sometimes never, use.

humility

There is a cliché about North Country people . . . they don't talk about much except the weather. It's a standard joke in books, movies and television shows.

You've seen it. The city slicker moves to the Northeast and encounters two grizzled old-timers at the local lunch counter:

"Cold, innit?"

"A-yuh."

"Gonna get colder."

"Likely."

These exchanges are seen as evidence of limited lives and intelligence. Before living here, I might have snickered with the rest of them at such country cuteness.

But the fact is, for us the weather is like a member of the family—an unpredictable family member at that. The temperamental uncle who drinks a little too much at weddings and must be watched with caution lest he disrupt the occasion. The cousin who causes an uproar with his escapades, the niece with her string of troublesome boyfriends, the cantankerous grandmother who speaks her mind at inopportune times.

The whole family lives on the edge of anticipation. It isn't a matter of *if* but *when* the next incident will occur. Just like the weather.

In other locales, life provides insulation from the elements. Here, it's personal. Public transportation doesn't ease us from place to place. That's my car buried under a foot of newly fallen snow. If I want to get anywhere, I have to deal with it.

Just try to flag a cab in the North Country.

Modern technology fails in the face of nature's force. Miles of electric lines are at the mercy of overhanging branches. In Ryegate, we rarely lose power altogether, but somewhere down the line a tree tapping a windy rhythm causes lights to flicker, and every flashing electronic gadget must be reset.

Even the satellite dish is subject to storm. A good hard rain or heavy snow sends it into a tizzy. On-screen entertainment is reduced to a single message: "Searching for satellite signal. Please stand by."

Please stand by. Weather-wise, we have a lot of that. Enough rain to fill your well? Please stand by. Will the foliage festival be blessed with sun? Will there even be leaves on the trees? Rain dates and "weather permitting" are standard fare, our bow to the inevitable beyond our control.

Maybe that's why country folk come across just a little more humble, a little more plain than their sophisticated city brethren. We have little opportunity to indulge in the illusion that we're in control.

We know our place.

We know we are not masters of our environment. We are subordinate to the whims of forces that affect every detail of our lives. Plumbing is a modern convenience most take for granted, but when the wind blows and electric lines become the stage for tap-dancing trees, you can't flush the toilet without the water pump.

And Uncle Albert may well tipple a bit too much at sister Susie's wedding.

Please stand by.

rural route blues

I know the Enhanced-911 system is a good thing. Emergency services people are in a hurry. Whatever gets them there quicker benefits us all.

And I don't want to belittle all the folks who've put in hundreds of frustrating, tedious hours naming roads, numbering houses, feeding endless lists of addresses into uncooperative computers.

But permit me, please, a sense of loss for my rural route address.

I am not a country girl born or bred. I have had street addresses most of my life. It was only when I moved to Ryegate Corner ten years ago that I received my rural route ranking.

Newly countrified, I encountered conflicts with most salesclerks when I ordered from catalogs.

"Box 132A, Rural Route 2," I'd say, and before I could get to my town and state . . .

"UPS won't deliver to post office boxes," they'd snip at me. "We need a street address."

"But it's *not* a post office box," I'd explain. "It's a rural route box. I can't give you a street address. We don't *have* them out here in the country."

It got so I'd get the jump on them and explain in advance,

before confiding my address. But every once in a while, a clerk would chuckle.

"You don't have to explain to me," they'd say with delight. "I grew up in the hills of Kentucky." Or the Virginia mountains, or Iowa farm country, or a little town in Texas . . .

Chatty conversations would follow. No matter how much they enjoyed their adopted city lives, they'd tell me their country stories with pride and affection.

"I'd like to go back when I have children," I'd often hear. "The city's fun, but I want my kids to grow up like I did. In the country."

They'd talk to me as if I were kin. Surprised at first, I gradually understood. I thought my small-town, rural Vermont life was unique. But country is country.

Across America, country folk are linked, pearls on a string of rural routes.

As metropolis turns into megalopolis and country is cornered by urban sprawl, rural folk feel like we're on the last outposts of a vanishing frontier. We're always happy to run into someone from home.

I didn't know so much was wrapped up in my rural route address until it was taken away.

"Please begin using this new address immediately," the form letter with my street designation commanded. And thus died the rural route, without fanfare. Too officious for me.

I need to believe in a place where the volunteer firefighters just know where I live. Where "the old Etta White place" is the only address I need. A place where neighbors' names are landmarks in the directions I give to my home.

I don't think I'm alone. Look at country music's explosive popularity. It's not just that you can hear the words and it has a good beat. Its appeal lies in what the words reveal, and the rhythm is the heartbeat of an American life we don't want to lose.

I hope someone writes a song. The Ballad of Rural Routes— a web of roads weaving together the country of our country. I'll sing along.

In Memoriam
RR2, Box 132A
Groton, Vermont

candles in the dark

In the wake of the September 11 attacks, thousands of personal stories continue to unfold. We see them on television; we hear them from friends and relatives. As I listen, I am all too aware of the stories we cannot hear from those we have lost.

Each story weaves itself into the fabric of these dark days. They come from around the corner and from around the world. Grappling to grasp the inconceivable, we reach out to one another.

Through cyberspace, many of us have intimate and instantaneous contact with people we would not otherwise have known—and we "speak" more often with family and friends than we would via expensive long-distance phone calls. The neighborhood now has no boundaries.

So when I see the streets of Bradford lined with flags, I think of my friend who lives in a small town in Tennessee. She drove to work one morning to find red, white, and blue bows tied to every stop sign.

I received the same email from friends in San Francisco and in Burlington. On Friday, September 14, at 7 P.M., it read, wherever you are, stop what you're doing and step outside with candles burning. It will be a gesture of acknowledgment to those lost, those still working to find them, a gesture of unity and resolve.

I imagined what this might look like in a city, and for a moment I wished I could stand with a host of others amid thousands of small flames burning.

The days passed with numbing news, one report worse than the next. By Friday, I am not even sure what day it is. By Friday, I have forgotten the email.

By Friday, we need to get out of the house, away from the television we cannot bear to watch but cannot turn off. We go to the Barge Inn in Woodsville, as we often do. We want a dinner we do not have to cook, but mostly, we just need to be out.

In the midst of dinner, from across the room, I hear Maren—our waitress and the daughter of the restaurant's owner—saying she's not sure if they have candles.

I remember.

Soon, seven of us stand outside, lighting our candles from one another's flames. Neil, Maren, four strangers, and myself. At first, we are self-conscious. But then we quietly talk about where we were when we first heard, and about the deaths of people we knew. We talk quietly about our national grief, about our fears for the days ahead.

It is strangely intimate. Strange, yet comforting. Cars honk as they pass. Somehow they, too, become a part of our circle.

Then one man says, "Let us pray." And it seems utterly natural to be standing there at the edge of the parking lot with heads bowed, together—religious affiliations unknown—as his spontaneous and heartfelt prayer washes over us.

We blow out our candles. But in our spirits, the flames remain.

in the old house

— fall —

ghosts

In our century-old farmhouse on five acres, we live with blessings bestowed by the old-timers who carved out a homestead from a verdant but harsh environment.

Without central heating, vinyl siding, or air conditioners, the old-timers found other ways to minimize the impact of the elements. They used common sense and weather wizardry with wisdom arising from their connection to the land.

Our house sits sideways to the road, an oddity to my suburban-bred sensibilities. The people of the land were more discerning than housing development designers. Situated as it is, the narrower side of the house meets the buffeting north wind—an asset I appreciate anew each December.

The front of the house overlooks an open meadow to the east. The back faces west, where the brook borders the forest. As the summer sun gathers afternoon intensity, the natural air-conditioning of water and woods insulates us from the heat. In the bare-branched winter, the house is warmed by the morning sun rising across the open meadow and by unshaded afternoon sunshine.

In the environmentally conscious 1970s, architects and builders began advertising house designs that make the most of the lay of the land, a trend that continues today. They tout such energy-efficient consciousness as if they've discovered a new science. North Country old-timers were way ahead of them.

When we first bought our house, I suffered from the arrogance of a "modern" mind. Certain odd, old-fashioned elements were immediately "improved." Some of the things we changed would have been better left alone. Through the seasons, I have come to understand that the rhymes and rhythms of an era past provide comfort and practicality.

I live amid a rich legacy of people before me who were poets of the land, and I have learned to listen.

The stereotype of simple, slow-speaking, slow-moving country hicks resistant to change belies a deeper, more enduring truth. The test of time is essential in a climate that tries the mettle of body and soul, in a region where wealth has always been abundant in nature and scarce in dollars.

I live with the ghosts of people who daily turned their hands to a range of tasks you'd need an army of carpenters, plumbers, mechanics, and home designers to perform today. They pondered and puttered, contemplated and cobbled together a life against all odds. And they held it together with forbearance beyond the reckoning of later generations, who have been nursed on the milk of instant gratification.

I am not unhappy to be haunted by these ghosts. In beam and barn board they teach me still, though they have long since been laid to rest.

My soul has been touched by their spirit, and my heart sings that it is so.

country reminders

We live on the edge of wildness.

I was hanging out clothes on the back porch when I caught a glimpse of something brown slinking through the woods. Though camouflaged by underbrush, the creature was clearly too small to be a deer, too large to be a fox. I suspected it was a coy dog or coyote.

As I peered in vain to get a clear view through the dense, green, leafy screen across the brook, I felt as if I was being watched. A sentry was patrolling his territory, keeping an eye on me—an intruder on his turf.

Sitting down among the flapping towels, I gazed out at the woods sweeping around the back of our house. I felt the force of its secret life.

We think we own this land. We think we are at the center of life here, but we merely hold small spaces against the tide of wilderness around us. Anyone who has cleared a piece of land in the North Country and tried to keep it open knows this well.

An aerial photographer once took pictures of our home and came by to sell them to us. From his bird's-eye view, the clearings around our house and our neighbors' homes were small interruptions in an expanse of field and forest.

As we go about the business of our days, it is easy to forget this. Wrapped in our cloak of *Homo sapiens* self-importance, it is easy to deafen ourselves to the whispers in the woods. Easy to ignore animal trails and burrows in the labyrinthine landscape we inhabit.

Sometimes we are unpleasantly reminded. We've lost three cats in nearly as many years. Healthy felines who simply went out and never came back. No furry corpses on the roads nearby, but coyotes scream in the night.

The dogs slip away from the discipline of our domain and return from their foray into the forest with faces full of porcupine quills.

Sometimes we are pleasantly reminded. One night, I find a large dragonfly on the screen door. It is so absolutely still, I wonder if it is dead. Iridescent wings fully spread, green-eyed head glittering in the porch light. I examine it in detail, then carefully open the door, slip inside, and get my camera. It is unmoved by my return, faces the flash without flinching. Come daylight, it is gone.

I awake early one morning and step quietly outside under lightening, predawn skies. A deer and I surprise each other as it munches on flowers just beyond my door. It is the *tallest* deer I've ever seen. Perhaps it just stretched its neck in our unexpected encounter, but in the flick of time before it flees, my impression is all long legs and height like a baby giraffe. With a flip of white-tailed alacrity, it turns and gallops down the yard, drumming hooves thundering after it is out of sight.

We live on the edge of wildness.

the storm

When the power went off during a spectacular storm last week, I filled a room with candles. Neil and I then sat back to watch the show.

Bolts of lightning were so silver-blue you had to quickly shut your eyes. Pink sheet lightning illuminated the whole sky like dawn's early light. Crashing explosions of thunder rocked our house to its foundations.

The animals gathered around. They don't like storms and huddle close or follow us from room to room should we rise. Their fear reminds me of my own childhood storm trembling. I remember my grandfather reassuring me that the fearsome thunder was only God bowling.

"That was a strike," he'd say, nodding sagely at an especially shattering round. Just as Granddaddy intended, I would be distracted from my fear, my imagination casting images of the Divine Bowling Alley.

It takes a lot of candles to barely light a room. But the soft golden glow quiets me from the inside out. The television is just a big black box, two flames reflected in its inky depths. The refrigerator does not hum.

Sitting in the tranquil radiance, I find myself envying my pre-electricity forebears. Without live current running through the wires, the house seems serene to its very core.

Disconnected, I feel my breathing slow. A restfulness steals through me like the luxuriant laziness of a leisurely soak in a warm bath. Despite the roar of thunder and crack of lightning, the haloed flames bestow peace.

We do not speak much, Neil and I, as we watch the wild night from our gently illumined room. An "ooh" or "ahh" at an especially wondrous display. A crooned phrase for a startled beast. And yet, we commune more intimately than words would allow.

Then the power surges on. The house leaps to life. Lightbulbs flare. The water pump resounds from the basement, echoing through the ductwork. Plugged in again, my pulse quickens with the call to action.

The candles fade, their magic lost in the glare. Edges are sharp. I see dirty spots on the carpet. The papers stacked on the kitchen table are in clear view. The refrigerator hums.

I rise with a sigh to blow out the candles. But somehow, instead, I turn off the lights. I return to the couch. Neil smiles. A shocking pink bolt splits the sky.

"Ooooooh," we breathe together.

Rumbling above, a tumultuous roll of thunder. The dogs look up at us, deep concern reflected in their eyes. I reach down to pat furry heads . . .

"Don't worry," I say softly. "It's only God bowling."

leaves dancing

The thermometer on my back porch registered below sixty at noon today. The sun broke through the clouds occasionally . . . brief, bright blessings in the early-September gloom.

Summer is passing. The cats come in at night now, as if to reassure themselves of their permanent place at hearth and home. Feline affection quotients rise in direct proportion to the drop in temperature.

Nestled among all the other still-green trees, one young maple on our land is always the first to turn. Today I notice its foliage is fuchsia, a shocking pink more shocking amid calmer cousins still wearing their summer clothes.

This tree is a leafy messenger, the herald of days to come. Of hillsides in Crayola colors, wanton in a wild dying beauty, the prelude to snow and cold and mud. The messenger carries a heavy burden.

But this is the time between. No longer summer, not yet truly fall, and today I saw the leaves dancing.

Summer leaves do not dance. Warm summer breezes rustle the leaves. Air wafting through the woods sounds like the distant rush of an ocean's ebb and flow. Summer storms tear through trees, flailing whole branches, tipping treetops in trunk-shuddering groans like muscles protesting unaccustomed exercise. The leaves go mad with movement.

But today, in this time between, I saw the leaves dance. On

tranquil trees, each leaf twitched and twittered, turning and twisting, quickening on quiet branches. A flock of leaves, like birds fluffing their feathers with shivers of motion.

If leaves could be said to be excited, today they were beside themselves with glee.

At my kitchen sink, I stopped mid-dish at the sight. Watching, I felt the delight of a child when the circus comes to town. In the rush of joy, the heaviness borne by the glorious messenger tree was lifted from me. In that moment, the "before the snow flies" agenda I'd begun to cart around was suspended.

The awareness of the cycle of seasons can be comforting— winter will come and go and once again fold into summer— but focusing on the future can also be a burden.

The dance of leaves reminds me that this time between is a season unto itself. With its own gifts and glories, a time with more to offer than the countdown to festive foliage. This time offers more than a winter preparation period, more than summer's last gasp. Neither summer nor fall, this time between does not even have a name to call itself. But as I watched leaves dancing, I resolved to honor it. I will not surrender this time to summer regrets, fall's promise, or winter's intimidation.

I will dance with the leaves the time between.

everywhere ain't here

If you missed last week's column, you don't know the details of my Labor Day fall. Suffice it to say, I'm still laid up with a badly sprained ankle and assorted aches.

I'm talking on the phone a lot, at all hours. My local friends keep me company throughout the day; the night shift is shared with my California friends. That three-hour West Coast difference is a blessing in my sleepless crippled state.

Given my fresh empathy for the lame and halt, I'm ready to launch a grassroots movement demanding drastically reduced phone rates for the housebound. Phone conversations are not a luxury when you're shut in. Healing is directly proportional to one's sanity, and whispering to the walls is not conducive to recovery.

But I digress.

I have a friend in San Diego who loves North Country anecdotes. Bob says they give him comfort, reassurance that somewhere life goes on with a personal quality absent from the fast-paced, bureaucratic detachment of his city. One ankle-aching night, I told him one of my favorite small-town stories.

We'd forgotten to renew the dogs' licenses. If you miss the deadline, you pay a fine. I happened to run into Marsha, our town clerk, and she got this faraway look in her eyes. Then she said, "You haven't been in to register Devin and Teddy, have you?" I thanked her and later that day scuttled down to her office to do so.

"Unheard of," Bob breathed reverently. Then he paused. "You know your town clerk's name?" he marveled.

Then he paused again.

"Your town clerk knows your *dogs'* names?" he exclaimed. When I relayed his response to Marsha, his appreciation struck a spark in us. A warm, fuzzy pride. The glimpse from Bob's outside view renewed our awareness of a simple fact . . .

Everywhere ain't here. Remember the old television show *Cheers*? It was a hit because people loved the idea of going to a public place "where everybody knows your name." Here, we have whole *towns* like that.

People do complain about small-town life. Everybody knows your business (and talks about it, too). There's a sense of confinement and restriction in the midst of such small circles. Granted. But sometimes, familiarity is a good thing.

Like this week . . . My laptop went into hissy fits again, while I was on deadline, of course. The nice folks at Woodsville's Paige Computer made an emergency house call, no extra charge, because they knew I couldn't drive.

Bob will love that one.

Given the mess the world's in, I can't help but wonder what a difference it would make if we knew our adversaries' names . . . and their dogs' names, too.

the furnace factor

It is September, and one morning it was forty outside but we didn't turn the furnace on. Never mind what the indoor temperature was, or that I saw my breath in the basement where I foolishly ventured to do morning laundry.

We didn't turn the furnace on because this is Vermont and this is September and it just isn't done.

We refuse to turn on the heat, as do many Vermonters. No matter that a couple of months from now we would no more let our thermostats drop below sixty than we would strip in public.

It's September. No self-respecting Vermonter will give in to the weather.

Turning on the furnace or firing up the woodstove for the first time is an act of surrender not taken lightly by hardy North Country folk. Forget Labor Day: Heating the house is the defining moment when summer ends. Until then, we bask in the afternoon heat and pretend the chilly mornings and evenings don't mean what we know they mean.

Turning on the heat is an admission that the seasons have shifted. Winter stalks us for real.

Then there's the winter wimp issue. Can you take it when the air turns chill? How cold can you get before you give in? Get used to it. It's going to get a lot colder than *this*. If you give in now and turn on the heat, how will you cope when it really gets cold? This is Vermont machismo, practiced equally by both genders.

If you do break down and turn on the heat in early September, you would never admit it in public, possibly not even to your closest friends. Doing so would entail a terrible loss of face. Your friends may also be shivering and burying themselves under not-yet-aired quilts, but if you admit to turning on the heat, they will never let you hear the end of it.

Twenty years later, you would be known around town as the-one-who-turned-on-the-furnace-in-September.

It is acceptable to complain about pulling out blankets, sweaters, and sweatpants. From morning to night, the weather dances from fall to summer to fall. You may grouse about this awkward time of the year when fall and summer clothes clutter closets and drawers.

But turn on the furnace you must not.

Having been steeped in this tradition by my native North Country neighbors for twenty years, I was stunned this week when *two* of my multigenerational, dyed-in-the-green Vermont friends admitted they'd turned on the heat.

The first confessor said so with a defiant lift of her chin, as if challenging her ancestors with every word.

The second apologetically explained she'd built a fire "just to take the chill off." (Not to actually heat the house, mind you, just to take the chill off.) But as we talked about this defiance of Vermont tradition, she gave me a sideways smile and said, "You know, as I get older, I care less about that, and more about being warm."

They say wisdom comes with age. It also comes with a little help from the cold.

the gift

The fine summer weather we were denied in strings of rainy, humid days is now bestowed upon us in September.

For several days, the sun has shone with the special golden glow of this time when leaves begin to turn. The wind is summer-warm. Absent is the chill kiss of winter to come.

I have been torn between pleasures. There is the joy of staying at home, windows and doors thrown open in a sweet orgy of fresh air made more delicious by winter whispers stalking my thoughts.

But there is also the impulse to jump in the car, crank the windows down, and hit the road. I ache to be out. Drunk with the wine of wanderlust served in goblets of crystal sunshine, spiced with the bouquet of changing leaves' enchantment, I cannot sit still.

So I have alternated my pleasures, puttering through chores at home and venturing abroad to accommodate the wild whims born of these startling September days.

One home day, I was running washer-dryer marathons to the basement. While blankets flapped on the clothesline, I went out into the meadow to gaze at the distant mountains. Sitting in the emerald grass, arms hugging my knees, I became aware of white wings flitting through the green around me.

I held my breath and held still.

White butterflies. The small angelic creatures flew, came to rest, and flew again. Perhaps a dozen of them, pristine wings lighting on blades of grass and leafy bushes. They performed a dance of flight, punctuations of purity on the good green earth.

Enchanted by their ethereal presence, my eyes burned with gathering tears of wonder. I am, perhaps, a hopelessly sentimental sap . . . beauty often moves me to tears. When words fail in the face of grace, tears speak.

Butterflies are rich in lore, legend, and metaphor. In some traditions they are symbols of divine inspiration. They are also recognized as totems for Nature herself. Because of their caterpillar-to-winged-creature transformation, in many cultures butterflies symbolize the process of creation.

The Aztecs believed butterflies were the happy dead who visited living relatives to assure them all was well.

I do not know which message the butterflies meant to bring. Were they whispering blessings? Or were Mom and Dad dropping by to say hi?

I do not know. It is enough that they came, like fairies dancing on the wind.

It is a sweet vision to hold close for darker times—the day the white butterflies came to me.

philosopher's stone

S omeone is stealing our rocks.
   I don't think this theft is destined for or worthy of headline news, but isn't it a puzzling bit of human behavior?

There's an old stone wall up on piece of our land beyond sight of the house. It draws the southwestern boundary of our property, and is a monument to farmers who once made more of the land than we ever will.

Like many old stone walls, only a shadow of its former glory remains. More rock pile than wall now, it whispers reminders of the practical, artistic genius who built a rhythm of stones outlining the land.

I suspect the wall was built to keep cows out of an orchard. Amid thorny puckerbrush, some ancient trees still bear fruit, though only deer gather the harvest now.

The end of the wall comes near a dirt road and it is there, while walking the dogs, we noticed that someone has been stealing the stones.

Like a small bomb crater, earth naked, the depression where a rock had lain was immediately obvious. No small stone this. Its footprint was some two feet wide, almost a foot deep. A quick check confirmed a rock of that size was nowhere to be seen. It had not merely rolled away. It was gone.

Who would steal a stone, and why? Who would mar the rhythm of the old wall's fallen rhyme?

In a world where so much is beyond our influence—screaming headlines and petty politics—the poetry of old stones soothes our sensibilities. The song of stones is patience, endurance. Of time measured in earth cycles, not sound bites. Of things that last, even as they tumble.

The stones stand, even as they sink deeper into the earth. Though covered with lichen, past their purpose, still their anthem rings, a hymn of human need married to nature's gifts.

The stones stand, and I am reminded that rocky obstacles in the field can be put to good use. Reminded that beauty can be wrought from practical need.

The stones stand and I believe.

Steal my stones, and still I will believe.

leaf liturgy

No matter how cranky or distracted, everyone I know pauses amid life's trials and tribulations to appreciate the beauty of foliage season.

Many North Country natives would rather give up hunting season than publicly admit their cantankerous home turf has a natural beauty that makes living here worthwhile. But these days, even they are walking around like kids with a Christmas-morning look in their eyes.

Familiarity may breed contempt, but when the trees perform their fall magic tricks, it doesn't matter how many seasons you've witnessed the transformation. Every year nature paints the trees in utterly unique compositions. I've heard grizzled, taciturn old-timers rejoice over reds, and have listened to reverent reflections on the ratio of gold to orange.

Unlike winter weather discussions, foliage critiques don't compare past with present. Natives will say, "There's never been a winter like the one of . . . ," but I've never heard anyone insist that one long-past fall puts all others to shame.

This is a region where people have memories an elephant would envy. A place where the present is measured by the yardstick of how-things-used-to-be and generally found wanting. But fall sprinkles a twinkling of foliage fairy dust, enchanting people into pure appreciation of the present.

When the wonderment of leaves is accompanied by startling-bright, summer-warm days, people are downright giddy. They meet and greet and chatter uncharacteristically, silly grins on normally reserved North Country countenances.

"How 'bout this?" they babble. "Isn't this something?"

In some ways, fall magic is better than Christmas. There are no presents to ponder and purchase, no big meals to plan and cook, no enforced intimacy with people one might not otherwise choose to sit down with. The gifts are free, require no wrapping, and are always a delightful surprise.

Those of us who live in the North Country are privileged to witness the full range of fall's glory. It is a present that continues to unwrap itself—from the first leaf that turns, through ending days when leaves fly thicker than snowflakes in a blizzard. Visitors get a snapshot . . . one scene in a panorama of beauty. For them, it's like seeing only one part of a movie. They might catch the thrill of the opening, interesting plot twists in the middle, or the exciting conclusion.

But only we get the whole adventure.

Fall is, no doubt, breathtaking to visitors, but every time I see a busload of leaf-peepers, I can't help feeling sorry for them.

I'm sure the foliage is worth the trip from places where nature doesn't throw this annual extravagant party. But it can't compare to watching the trees put on their daily show of ever-changing hues.

"You are so blessed to live here," a recent visitor told me in dulcet tones of undisguised envy.

I opened my mouth to catalog the vicissitudes of winter, the limitations of life in the country, then closed it again.

"Yes," I finally said with a smile. "I am."

the lone hollyhock

In those glorious days last week when summer kissed fall good-bye, I began cleaning out the gardens.

I had modest ambitions. The sedum was in full magenta flower. The asters called bees to their spiky blooms. But in my gardens run rampant, these beauties were crowded by their dead and dying neighbors. I wanted to clear space around their final fall vibrancy.

There is something pathetic about summer flowers gone by. Bee balm stalks still stand straight and true, but their naked brown heads evoke memories of butterflies long gone.

The thistle's blue has passed its prime, sharp-edged leaves faded and wilted. Stalwart soldiers of the garden, they are battle-worn and silvered like old vets valiantly marching on parade.

Messiest are the daylilies. Green leaves tangle with crisp, brown, twisting dead threads and yellow strands. The once-proud stalks on which blooms bragged bright orange are now rigid, beige hollow tubes.

It is hard to honor my initial ambitions. I find myself working stretches far from the sedum and asters . . . Getting down into the rich, bare earth is deeply satisfying. I rip at invading myrtle. The loamy scent of damp soil is a musky perfume. Hypnotic.

When I was decades younger, I could clear a length of garden in a day. Now my knees scream.

I am not a total fool, however. I take frequent breaks, facing the woods where maples glow in yellow-gold-orange profusion. The trees are backlit by the late-afternoon sun. I am awash in a sea of golden radiance as the wind moves through the leaves like a gently rushing tide.

It would take a better poet than I to capture the smell of raw earth and leaves already composting on the grass, spiced by the pungent bergamot of newly cut bee balm. Such a heady mix, enough to drive a perfumer mad. Worth a fortune if bottled for the winter comfort it would give.

When I have done all I can do, I step back to survey my work outside the wall that runs along the road. Stripped to bare earth in some places, the long garden sports lingering green in others, and one tall stalk standing like an exclamation point.

It is a lone hollyhock.

Somehow, through the first frost and hard fall rains, a single pink flower trumpets from the top of the stalk.

Its bloom delicate, the blossom sings of summer. A frill in contrast with the sedum's chunky heads and the asters' spiky petals.

Pink and frivolous, she chimes fairy notes against the earth tones of fall.

She dances on the swaying stalk, gleefully defiant, playful. Days later, when the rain comes and wind blows the golden sea from the trees, she remains.

What garden magic this is, a sparkling touch from summer's wand.

farewell, well

We need a new well. After a long dry summer, we're certainly not alone. As we wait for the well drillers to fit us into their busy schedule, we count our blessings. The old dug well—down the hill, across the brook, and in the woods—hangs on with some twenty-nine inches of water. It's paper plates and quick showers at our house, but the toilets are still flushing.

It is the end of an era.

Our house was built in 1840. We suspect the well is as old as the house, and that's not just our opinion. Some years back, a mason came to repair the brick above ground level. "Haven't seen one like this," he said. "Has to be over a hundred years old." The plumber agrees.

For a city boy and a suburban girl, it is a strange and awesome thing to have a well. Growing up, we never thought much about water. Turned on the tap and there it was. We were not country kids. We made no connection between rainfall and the water we used.

Living with a dug well brought us into an intimate relationship with nature. Many's the summer we've prayed for rain. Walking in the woods always included a side trip; we'd lift the heavy well cover and check the water level. Respecting natural resources comes easily when you watch your water source change—you *see* the need to adjust your consumption.

We have felt closer to the land because of this.

Our dug well also brought dowsers into our lives. Go ahead and laugh, disbelievers. But several years back, when we were down to only eighteen inches of water, a dowser diverted a new vein into the well. We watched the water come up to ground level over the next two (rainless) days. That fix held steady for years.

When this summer's dry days stretched on, the water level dropped to about four inches. Another dowser came, diverted another vein that raised it to the present twenty-nine inches—enough to limp along. But, he said, that's as good as it will get because there is no other "mother lode" vein to feed the well.

"The veins are old and tired," he said.

When the well drillers set their bit to the ground, it will be in a dowser- recommended spot.

Once upon a time, some settlers trooped out into the woods, located the source, and dug that well—with picks and shovels, no doubt. We are awed by the fact that, more than a century later, their labor has sustained us for all these years.

So we're a little sad at the end of this era. Sentimental about breaking our link to the past. We won't miss dry-season, water-watchdog routines, and a worry-free water supply will be a luxury. But an artesian well will bring an elemental change to the old homestead.

After more than a hundred years of service, the dug well deserves to retire. "The water veins feeding it are old and worn," the dowser said. That's easy to believe.

But we let her go with sad gratitude. We tip our caps to the old-timers whose labors served us long after they were gone . . . They gave us more than water.

the great well-drilling adventure

I know I should be counting my blessings, and I am . . . but not without a few grumbles tossed in.

Out of Lyndonville, the good men from Goulds came. They delicately positioned a humongous drilling rig between our house, the rock wall, and the crab apple tree as if it were a Volkswagen bug neatly tucked into a tight parking spot. The drill shaft towered above our two-story home, with mere inches of clearance between it and the eaves.

The artistry of men and big rigs is a wonder to behold.

There's something very special, too, about talking with men about work they love. John Gould and his son (also named John) revealed the mysteries of water. They spoke of slate and shale, granite and quartz, and the geological reasons why water pools where it does.

I cannot remember all the details. What I remember is the animated way they talked, their enthusiastic fascination with their craft. I remember son John's almost affectionate description of his quartz collection—jars of jewels from the earth, rainbows of rock.

The Goulds were receptive to the advice of our dowser, Dave Royer of Orleans. "I've seen 'em hit it right on, I've seen 'em be totally wrong," the elder John said. The exact well location was determined through a harmonious blend of Dave's arcane art of dowsing from a distance, Neil's and my on-site dowsing, and the Goulds' technical know-how.

Dave said we'd find seven gallons a minute below two hundred feet, but above three hundred. At 260, we hit six gallons a minute.

Everyone was happy.

Before the Goulds could install the pump and run water into the house, they were called to answer a water emergency. Our old well was giving us enough to hang on, so we didn't begrudge the delay while they responded to the needs of the waterless. But for four days, our yard looked like a mini-strip-mining operation—complete with slag piles and yawning pits of scummy water.

We were grateful when they returned. Finally, after two days of flushing brown and heavily chlorinated water through our pipes, I'm happily doing long-delayed laundry at home, with nary a worry about the well. I'm savoring the new quiet of a water pump buried deep in the earth rather than loudly resonating from our basement.

But we're surrounded by a moat of mud, from the north end of the house, up our driveway, and along the full length of the front yard. It's going to be a looong winter. We'll be hoping for deep snows. Otherwise, it will be months of mucky dog paws and mire tracked into the house.

Change is not neat and tidy. If you dig deep, you're going to make a mess. The alternative is to limp along with an antique well long past its prime.

Better to get down to deep waters, where the flow is fresh, pure, and plentiful.

trick or treat, please

Living off the beaten path in the North Country makes Halloween a chancy affair. Some years we get a clutch of kids. Other years there have been none. But still, every year I buy candy in hopeful anticipation . . . and with practicality.

I always choose candies I like. I may have to eat them.

As Halloween looms, I feel like a kid when Christmas approaches—all aflutter to catch a glimpse of Santa or hear reindeer on my roof. Not knowing what gifts might appear makes pre-Christmas the most magical time. Anything, everything is possible. With delight, I imagine each prospect in delicious detail.

It is in this spirit that I await Halloween. What might show up at my door? Fairies? Bums? Witches or princesses? Ghosts, goblins, or gory ghouls?

The young ones are so cute, tripping over hastily hemmed costumes. They often turn shy at my door, but I've heard their boisterous laughter as they scamper back down my driveway. Excitement barely repressed—they're out at night!

Some Halloweens are bitter cold and snowy. Little ballerinas arrive wrapped for warmth, gauzy tutus peeking out of winter coats. Earmuffs snuggle under princesses' tiaras.

I was once visited by an infant mouse swaddled in a fuzzy cocoon, held in Mother's arms. Wide-eyed with whiskers delicately drawn on baby skin . . . we're never too young for fun.

Nor are we ever too old. Some parents play along with their kids. From a simple witch's hat to Broadway-elaborate creations, grown-ups bring their thrills to my door.

Teenagers come with a swagger declaring they're just out for a lark, but their eyes shine with a child's joyous spark. You're not fooling me, I want to whisper. I know some of your friends must say it's not cool—but I'm glad you're not letting them make the rules.

Some years I lined up my pumpkins, turned on the outside lights, and did not see one trick-or-treater throughout the lonely night. It's the silliest thing, but I feel so sad . . . as if I missed a party the other kids had. I don't care how much candy I get to eat—the evening is empty of the very best treat.

I console myself with chocolate, but I only want more . . . I want the night's magic that didn't stop at my door.

So next year, please put on your costumes and come to my house . . . I'd even be happy with one baby mouse.

imperfect apples

At the edge of the meadow beyond our house stand two ancient apple trees. The bark of each is nearly black, and rough like the leathered skin of lifetime farmers too much in the sun.

The trees are not graceful. Dead and gnarled branches reach skeletal arms in all directions and clack in the wind, as if possessed . . . haunted creatures from a Stephen King story.

The apples grow on high, impossibly out of reach. Gravity plucks them for us, tossing them to the cushioned, grassy ground.

Every other year, the trees bear beautifully. Ankle-deep in apples, we stumble amid the windfall. We choose the best, leaving for wildlife those already sampled by deer. They seem to nibble once and move on, shopping for the sweetest spot among the lot.

Like the trees that bear them, the apples are flawed. Often oddly shaped, always blemished and bruised from their rough harvest. Many have a small circle of exposed flesh, as if some tiny insect has sampled a delicate bite.

If these imperfect apples were stacked in a store, I would pass them by. I would be indignant at the notion that I should pay good money for such unattractive specimens. But at home, I happily gather them in the morning, still cold from the ground.

Peel away the blemishes and the bruises are shallow, easily sliced off. Where insects have sampled, there is no trace. Once I have done my magic with the knife, what remains is white, unflawed fruit.

If beauty is only skin-deep, then so, too, are many defects and deformities.

Beneath their unattractive exterior, the apples present a gift. Untouched by chemicals, untrucked and safely stored in nature's night-cool refrigerator, this backyard bounty offers a taste and vibrant freshness that triumphs over their perfect brethren.

I do not know what kinds of apples fall from our trees. I suspect they are old-time species that do not lend themselves to mass cultivation. One is dark ruby and neither soft nor firm. It is sweet, but with a slight tang. The other is pale with red streaks, tart and crisp. Even in California where I've encountered apples I've never seen elsewhere, none are like ours.

Apple growers are not to blame. They must produce what the market will bear, and even I have arrogantly demanded perfect apples when money is laid down.

This makes me wonder what trade-offs we make for perfection.

If there were blemished apples in our stores, would children still diet themselves into ill health and request nose jobs for Christmas?

Would we vote for the politician with the best ideas instead of the best hair?

Would bald men stop spending a fortune for hair transplants?

Would women find happiness with bodies that take shape naturally and turn away from the surgeon's knife?

A heavy burden of thought to lay upon a simple apple, perhaps. But my mind does wander as I peel my imperfect apples.

a little less country

One day recently, there was a commotion just beyond our house. Up at the corner where the dirt road leads down to Marsha and Fremont's farm, a bunch of trucks had gathered and men were milling around.

The dogs went berserk, as they do when anyone crosses the invisible canine boundaries that mark their territory. Barking and growling, they ran from kitchen to living room, then sped through the house rounding up their human charges to defend the homestead.

Neil and I came from opposite ends of the house. We met in the middle amid the flying fur of boisterous beasts. On our way to the kitchen rendezvous, we noticed the peaceful assembly at the corner.

We were not alarmed. But to settle the dogs down, the clan must gather. We must look out the windows, acknowledge the interlopers, praise the sentries' vigilance, and finally tell the troops they can stand down.

As we performed the obligatory window watch, Neil and I could not at first see why the men and machines had congregated. Then it arose, startling against the naked landscape of late fall.

A silver pole gleaming unnaturally against the vista of hill and dale, precise white letters glaring from a green background unlike any green produced by nature . . .

It was a street sign.

The pole, uniformly round. The sign, geometrically rectangular. It stood stark against the overlapping lines and curves of the countryside.

It's the strangest sight I've seen in some time. A thing so patently out of place, like donkeys gathered in a high school gym for a laughable basketball game.

I am not unfamiliar with street signs. I've lived in places where they abound and have taken no more notice of them than I do of fall leaves drifting to the ground. Street signs are associated with suburban housing developments and the concrete corridors of cities. I am accustomed to them also in our small towns, where handfuls of streets have agreed to meet between acres of open land.

But in the country? Street signs? We don't even *have* streets out here, not really—we have roads. A whole 'nother thing altogether.

I am aware that our new street signs are benevolent. They will guide emergency personnel more swiftly to save lives and property from catastrophe. But the signs just look funny.

Silver poles among towering pines. Street names at the head of unpaved paths into the forest where a single house nestles out of sight. Weird. Signs speaking along meandering back roads where, before, nature whispered wordlessly. Strange.

I have a sneaking suspicion that when my city friends read this column, they'll shake their heads at the image of two adults and two dogs gathered intently at the window to watch a street sign go up. They'll tell me I really have to get a life.

Maybe I'll just ask them what they'd do if three or four guys pulled up in trucks outside their apartment windows and proceeded to plant a full-grown pine tree next to their subway stop.

street signs
and country roads

I still have street signs on my mind. I keep thinking about how many changes the signs portend.

Since moving to the North Country some twenty years ago, I've noticed that every time someone asks for directions, an oral history is created and maintained. In this simple act, the life of a town is chronicled, communicated, and registered in the unwritten archives of the community.

"Go over the bridge and past the big brown barn. That used to be the Fuller farm, but old Jake hurt his back and sold out when I was a kid. There was a fire there last year. Fire department got there real quick, but you can still see where the trees burned . . .

"Then go a quarter mile past the beaver pond. It flooded but good and washed out the road last spring. Road crews fixed it up fast so folks could get to town meeting, but the debris is still piled up. You never smelled such a stink as when that beaver dam broke."

Where there are back roads, stories are shared. I've overheard our home's history recounted in location conversations like this:

"They live just up from the corner at the old White place."

"That's the one with the rock wall running along the road?"

"Yup. They built that wall after a drunk drove right into their living room."

"I remember hearing about that. Nobody was hurt, as I recall."

"Nope. They will be next time if somebody drives into that wall. Took three truckloads of stone and ninety bags of mortar to put it up. Ran their well dry mixing the mortar."

"That was the summer of the drought, wasn't it? Farmers hauled water from the river for their herds . . ."

So it went. Now it will go like this:

"Take a left at Witherspoon. They're the last house on the left before Scotchburn."

Will the stories be lost? What else will be lost now that there are mapped solutions for what used to be the puzzle of back-country roads?

There has always been a certain mystery on back roads. It has been a favorite fair-weather rite to follow them just to see where they lead. We took a dirt-road drive one day from Ryegate and ended up in St. Johnsbury by a route I could not describe even under torture. But we found beautiful places buried in the hills: farms and ponds and fancy houses we never knew existed behind forest curtains.

Sometimes, it's more fun not to know where you're going. It's a treat to wander where the only traffic is a farm truck or two, where only back-road residents travel the labyrinth of lanes winding through the woods.

With every road mapped and named, the secret will be out. We'll lose that sense of adventure I've always found so sweet.

"You can't get there from here" may become an obsolete phrase now that street signs mark the way.

In a world of turmoil and trouble, this is a small loss. But permit me to ponder, with sentimental regret, the day street signs came to the country.

lasting leaves

E ven the unflappable old-timers concede that this fall's refusal to surrender to winter's domination is unusual. I haven't heard one of them say, "A-yuh, but this is nothin' compared with the year . . ."

It's mid-November and everyone's talking about leaves.

As I write, snow falls lightly on russet foliage. It's the third time we've had a dusting, and the leafy phenomenon continues to the delight of North Country citizenry.

The stubborn leaves are a fascinating gift. As long as the trees aren't bare, we can pretend the snow is an aberration of late fall rather than a sign of early-onset winter.

If this just sounds like word games, you've never lived in this neck of the woods. You must be a distant friend or relative who receives our hometown paper to keep up with Johnny's basketball team.

Here in the North Country, anything that keeps winter at bay is a blessing.

Nature's standard practice goes like this . . . After peak foliage weekend, early in October, a hard and windy rainstorm usually sweeps the leaves from the trees in one fell swoop. That's it—the swan song of fall. One day, the trees are dressed in all their final glory. The next morning, we're confronted by skeletal branches scrabbling into leaden skies.

It's a sad day, heralding the interminable cycle of winter

and mud season ahead. We take a deep breath and psychologically dig in for the long haul. Faces get a little grimmer, footsteps get a little slower as folks shoulder the burden of what's-to-come.

Customarily, we've hoisted the winter millstone by Halloween. This year, instead, people are merrily talking about the leaves.

This year, trick-or-treaters had to bundle up against the cold, but they skipped down streets where maples still glowed golden in carved-pumpkin candlelight. Weeping willows waved them on their way with unseasonably green and graceful branches, ghostly arms in the twilight.

On Election Day, Ryegate was a study in winter picture-postcard, snow-frosted, pine-tree perfection . . . with lingering touches of foliage dressing.

I bet some naturalist could explain why the leaves have triumphantly sustained assaults by wind, rain, sleet, and snow. It might be interesting to find out—but no explanation would change my utter delight.

Science would not dull the unexpected magic of sunshine on snow-kissed hillsides while green still fills the blanks between bare trees. Facts would not blunt the joy walking beneath not-yet-bare branches, shuffling my feet through freshly fallen leaves while catching icy flakes on my tongue.

Even if today's storm forces the leaves into a final winter surrender, I will feel this strange November lightheartedness.

I have been spared a month of stark, leafless landscapes.

Despite the north wind's early bitter cold and snows, the Winter Witch has been cheated—just a bit—from her usual wicked grip.

winter weirdos

I woke this morning to powdered sugar frosting every leaf and limb . . . and contemplated winter slipping onto center stage.

The very thought of the months ahead tightens my jaw and sets my spirit in grim determination against battering elements to come. Once again, we will be at the whim of weather. The best-laid plans subject to disruption by icy roads.

Baby, it will be cold outside. The indolence of warmth will wrap itself around us, keeping us cuddled close at home.

Going and doing becomes as complex as maneuvers in a military campaign. The weapons of winter—scarves and scrapers, boots and battery warmers—will clutter closets and hallways. Mothers with children will plot strategies a general would envy to get tiny troops outfitted for the field.

If we had the good sense of our forest friends, we wouldn't fight the lassitude of winter. We'd simply hunker down in our caves and hibernate till spring.

And yet, in each of us who chooses to live here, there must be some whisper of winter running through our veins. Something that secretly celebrates the still solitude of the season. What other explanation is there for our voluntary surrender to a climate such as this? Here, where spring, summer, and fall combined barely match the number of months in winter's grasp?

Winter's quietude holds us with its spell. Were it not for our willingness to be so entranced, surely we would have left long ago.

I remember a conversation some years back, just as the last snows retreated into deep forest shadows. We were sighing, a farmer friend and I, at the prospect of all the fair-weather chores ahead. Of fields and flowers to be tended, of dry roads and social obligations. Eyes shifting, voices lowered to protect our confessions, we were a secret sisterhood of spring regret.

"I'm just not ready to give up winter," she whispered.

"I know," I commiserated. "I'll miss the quiet."

Unbeknownst to us, another friend had moved within hearing. Her winter-crazed cackle gave her away, and we turned to see her gaping at us in disbelief.

"You guys," she pronounced, "are crazy."

She backed away as if we might infect her with our madness.

Alone again, we shrugged and smiled. Unspoken images of a countryside hushed with snow danced between us, the tang of wood smoke in the air.

Crazy? Maybe. But I suspect that here in the North Country, confessed or not, there are others like us.

Others who embrace winter grace.

when progress isn't

I have scrupulously avoided addressing our presidential un-election. I figure folks get bashed by hard news from other sources—I do my small part to provide a peaceful alternative to shouting headline issues.

However, a few small-town perspectives occurred to me, so I'm going to plunge into the election mire with two cents clutched in my grubby journalistic paw.

What got me started was an article in *The New York Times*. They interviewed the makers of various automated voting systems. Each and every one of these experts flat-out said that manual counting of votes is more reliable than machine counts. The *standard margin of error* in their machines, they pointed out, is modest in proportion to the numbers of votes cast . . . but in this election, it could determine who moves into the White House.

They hastened to add that in most elections, erroneously tabulating a few hundred votes doesn't make a difference. Not so now. They advocated manual recounts of *all* ballots in areas where results were close.

The voting machine experts say research has repeatedly proven hand counting is significantly more accurate than automated tallies.

Didn't that make me smile.

Even before personal computers became common household items, there have been people who predicted that, one day, machines would take over the world. They were laughed at.

In our present mishmash, regardless of who is declared the winner, I'll wonder who really elected the man. A president of the people, elected by the people—or brought to us courtesy of machine margin of error.

By contrast, I thought about voting here in the North Country. I troop into the town hall and get my ballot from Beulah, who recognizes me on sight and checks me off the list. We exchange pleasantries. I go into the voting booth, pick up a pencil, and put my mark in the appropriate boxes. If I have any questions about the ballot, I just peer out from behind the curtain and ask.

When I've finished, I fold up my ballot, stuff it in the wooden box, and get my name checked off again.

After the polls close, a bunch of people I know open the box, sit down, and count the votes. It's a big job, and they deserve lots of credit for their efforts. Some ballots are hard to read, no doubt, with incompletely erased changes. Those confusions are a whole lot simpler to resolve, however, than deciding when a punched hole is not punched enough.

There are no chads, pregnant or otherwise, up here in the North Woods.

So here's what I think. Everyone should pick up a pencil and vote. And those votes should be counted by living, breathing human beings. We may be flawed, but we're better than machines.

Just ask the guys who make and market the suckers.

winter gardening and remembering george

Courtesy of an errant jet stream, I happily tug and cut the last bits of dead growth from my garden. The wind is cool but not raw. The sun dances in and out of fluffy clouds; the brook sings merrily in the background.

It is the first day of December.

From the Pacific Northwest to Arkansas, people are buried in snow and slipping on icy roadways. Our turn will come—perhaps by the time this column appears. But for now, our unusual Indian summer has become an amazing Indian winter, and I'm doing yard work.

I opened a few windows before grabbing my pruning shears and cranked up the stereo. The last of the phlox fell to the tunes of *Rubber Soul*.

George Harrison is dead.

As pungent yarrow spices the air, I wonder how Ringo and Paul feel. There were four, then in a shocking moment there were three—now there are two. I hope they hold each other tight. I hope they cry.

In the wake of 9/11, I do not mourn George as if his loss is more significant than terror's victims or the casualties of war. This is simply different.

With George's passing, memories flash across my mind. I am

just thirteen. My boyfriend's name is, coincidentally, George. Our song is "We Can Work It Out." I still remember all the words.

I still remember how thrilling it was to dance in a bear hug just out of the chaperones' view. Yes, Virginia, there was a day when dances were chaperoned, and imperious hands would insist on a palm's-width distance between young bodies.

My generation was not the first to mark memorable moments with music. Bobby-soxers screamed and fainted for Sinatra at the Paramount a generation before Elvis, long before the Fab Four shook their mop tops at screeching girls, courtesy of Ed Sullivan. I never understood how grown-ups could be quite so disapproving of Beatlemania, given the fabled hysteria of young Sinatra fans.

I grew up with the Beatles. I watched the Beatles grow up. In the turbulent '60s, when everything was changing faster than lightning, the dapper suits they brought across an ocean gave way to beards and beads and all manner of strange dress. The simple chords of "She Loves You" took a magical mystery tour by way of Eastern mysticism—largely thanks to the quiet Beatle—and we stopped guessing what the boys would come up with next.

We just knew we'd be listening.

More decades later than I care to count, I am on the opposite coast from where I first put a Beatles album on a turntable. A remastered CD resonates from speakers I could not have imagined back then, bringing "Norwegian Wood" from my house into the garden at the edge of these New England woods, on a remarkable December day . . . while I remember George.

Isn't it good?

confession

Our remarkably mild November was surprise enough here in the North Country, but December's Indian summer strained the bounds of believability.

With the cold airstream stalled somewhere over Canada, we enjoyed weather we'd be lucky to have in May. Prudently donning hunter-orange caps, Neil and I walked in the woods with our jubilant dogs. The ferns were still green among fallen leaves.

The primroses in my garden were confused, reaching out with new leaves in the unseasonable warmth. We pondered our choices in the Christmas tree lot without the customary ache of cold toes to hurry us along.

I opened windows, relished the silent oil furnace, and left the fire laid but unlit. Even as I gloried in this and rejoiced in the freedom to go and do unhampered by winter weather, I was unsettled.

No matter how I counted the blessings of balmy days, the naked brown branches and leaf-strewn ground dragged at my spirits. Just as I was getting into the swing of the holiday season, I was distracted by temperate days.

There are always fall chores left undone. Once the cold and snow arrive, we let them go with relief . . . But this year, leftover fair-weather tasks could still be undertaken. Those demands clashed with impending Christmas chores.

Then everything changed. On Monday, December 7, the thermometer at the north end of the back porch registered nearly seventy in early afternoon. Within hours, I watched the temperature drop twenty degrees. By nightfall, it was cold enough to light a fire. On Tuesday, it snowed.

The countryside is transformed by a dusting of snow. No matter how long I live here, no matter how often I see it, it's magical. Harsh lines of skeletal brown branches are softened. Dead leaves are blanketed, hidden from sight.

All is clean and pure and peaceful.

Grumbling about the trials of winter is a time-honored tradition. Meeting the challenge of snow and ice is a source of secret pride, the steel in Yankee spines. But appreciation of winter's calm is a deeper secret still.

I am not alone in welcoming winter's maiden snowfall. The storm caught me in St. Johnsbury, shopping at the bookstore. Back in the stacks, I missed the first flakes.

"Ohhhh," I heard a breathless customer exclaim, "it's *snowing*."

There was a rustle throughout the store as people turned to the windows and passed the word, delight ringing in each voice.

Café clatter hushed. Cash registers stopped clicking. Grown-up, weekday shoppers turned into kids before my eyes. Faces lit with enchantment.

Winter's here.

football fellowship

I have this thing about football. A well-timed tackle is sweetly satisfying. When the quarterback lets loose a long one arcing down the field like a homing device into the outstretched arms of a receiver who dances into the end zone, it's purely a thing of beauty.

But I couldn't tell you who's injured this week, or how many games a team has to win to have a shot at the Super Bowl. And while I have a sentimental affection for the San Francisco 49ers, I follow no particular team with passion.

I generally root for the underdog. The excitement of surprise thrills me: valiant David toppling Goliath in front of deliriously cheering fans. I just like to see a good contest, no matter who's playing.

Blame it on my dad, this love of the game.

In his college years, Dad was a sports announcer. He knew football. The history of players and teams, and in those days before on-field microphones he translated the referees' arm-waving signals for me.

My mother and sister were not seduced by the siren song of pigskin. Watching football, I had Dad to myself.

Dad hated chatty announcers. He'd bring the portable television up from their bedroom and set it next to the console TV in the living room. Turning off the sound, he'd announce both games, complete with background history and stats for players and teams.

I cannot watch a football game without feeling close to Dad, though he's been gone now for over a decade.

One recent Monday night, I wandered over to the Shaeffer Stadium in Woodsville after a frustrating day at the keyboard when words would not bend to my will. I hadn't planned on more than a quick dinner and a quiet drink before heading back to the word wars.

But I ran into some friends there, die-hard Patriot fans, gathered for the game against the Dolphins. Before I knew it, I was wrapped in the magic of football fellowship.

Like Dad, they knew football. I heard the stats and stories between plays—the only time it is acceptable to talk with men watching football. I found out why Boomer was on the announcer's team, and why Frank Gifford had left.

We watched and whooped and hollered. By ten thirty, I was the only female left in the place. A technicality really: I wasn't female anymore; I was just a football fan.

It was a great game. A nail-biter to the very end, filled with high drama. Interceptions, bad calls that worked both for and against us, broken plays and perfect plays choreographed like ballet.

The tensions I'd walked in with had dropped away. It was a different world. A world of pleading, exhorting, cursing, and celebrating figures flickering on screens all over the room.

Bledsoe injured his fingers in the final moments of the game, so when he tossed the ball for the Patriots' winning touchdown with only seconds to spare, we all exploded from our seats in sheer joy.

Sheer joy. Football fellowship.

Thanks, Dad.

all the news that's
fit to burn

The recent combination of arctic cold and the high cost of heating oil have brought me into intimate interaction with our wood-burning furnace.

In keeping with fine North Country tradition, this furnace is not a high-tech wonder. Its brand name, if it had one, would be *Jury-rigged*. It consists of a three-quarter-inch steel firebox lined with firebrick, encased in sheet metal.

Don't laugh. Before we upgraded the original, its heart was an old oil drum.

Like much of life in our rural environment, this setup is simple but functional, powerful but not easily mastered, efficient but cantankerous. You do not just load her up and leave her be. She demands constant care and feeding.

If you do the job right, and the north wind doesn't howl down off the hill too maniacally, you might get two hours between tendings.

She resides in the basement, a trek down two flights if I'm on the second floor when duty calls. At the bottom of the steep, narrow basement stairs, there's a door to be opened, then a left turn, a step down, another door, a narrow path around the oil furnace, and finally there's the wood furnace.

The furnace opening would challenge a Munchkin. Even for

one of my petite stature, the steel door just above floor level requires crouching on one's haunches while holding heavy hunks of wood and, from this precarious position, shoving them into the furnace's insatiable maw. A full loading routine then requires standing, turning to heft another log from the woodpile (being careful not to bonk heads with the conveniently located septic pipe), and crouching again to strategically place the wood according to the furnace's persnickety requirements.

So it goes. Endlessly. You can understand why, contrary to conventional wisdom, I lose weight in the winter.

Given the consequences of failure, it's critically important to get the fire off to a good start. This involves lots of scrap hardwood and stacks of newspaper.

The burn quality of newspapers varies as much as their editorial content. For those wood-heating neophytes among us, I offer the following observations . . .

The *Times Argus* goes up in a flash, with little effect and much fire-smothering debris. *The Caledonian-Record* is only slightly better at generating heat and produces an equal amount of undesirable residue. *The Burlington Free Press* burns with more substance and reduces more neatly. The *Journal Opinion* is one notch better still on both counts.

But the Sunday *New York Times* is the newspaper to be reckoned with. This is a paper with substance. It burns hot and slow and clean. It's a newspaper fire-starters can love.

Whatever other merits these newspapers may have, it's the *JO* and the *Times* I want stacked next to our wood furnace.

Not the ringing endorsement the publishers have in mind, no doubt. But this is winter in a hundred-plus-year-old North Country farmhouse, and we do have our priorities.

keeping up with
the joneses

Neither of my nearest neighbors has the last name Jones. And conventionally, this expression implies a superficial, materialistic competitive spirit. Your neighbor buys a new car, you buy a new car—probably a flashier car.

I'm not naive. There are places where people really do feel this pressure to keep up appearances, to play along with a standard of acquisitiveness set by their community. I just don't think it's a signature of life in the North Country.

The North Country version of "keeping up with the Joneses" seems to be a delightfully positive phenomenon. I can't speak for others, naturally; this is just how it is for me.

Small-town life simply makes everything a little more personal.

In the spring, gardens gracing yards along the road to my house feel like extravagant presents. I know they weren't planted for me, but I take such pleasure in them. This inspired me to plant my own garden along the wall that borders our road. Hokey as it sounds, I felt I was adding a touch of beauty to my town. I wanted others to experience the pleasure they gave me—drive-by gifts, random acts of beauty in bloom.

Keeping up with the Joneses.

Ours is one of three houses just beyond the heart of Ryegate Corner. We're good neighbors by North Country standards. We don't disturb one another. We're courteous on the rare occasion when we might ask for a favor. The night of the lunar eclipse, I asked Dave to turn off his floodlights. He cheerfully complied. When Steve had a family reunion, we were happy to allow our meadow to become their parking lot and playground.

In an unspoken but generous manner, we acknowledge that our proximity to one another means we're immediately affected by each other's activities.

Just after Thanksgiving, my neighbors declared the opening of holiday season with lights. I was inspired to do my own decorating. Keeping up with the Joneses? In a way. They'd given me something beautiful to look at. They brought dancing lights to the dark days of December.

I wanted to return the favor.

There's a symmetry to the Christmas lights, now, in this trinity of homes. I look out my front porch, past the sparkling tree Neil and I put up there. Across the meadow, through Steve and Lori's sliding glass door, I see a cascade of white lights. Beyond that are the colored lights on the chubby pine tree in Dave and Debbie's yard.

Perhaps I am a sentimental sop. But these strings of light weave a sense of community for me. Here on this stretch of country road, three houses adorn the night—each separate and distinct, together singing a visual holiday chorus to people driving by.

After more than twenty-five years in the North Country, small-town life still surprises and delights me. Its qualities do not fade with familiarity; they deepen with each passing year.

a holiday tale

I've never had an artificial tree. Even when I lived in California and a Christmas tree cost more than some of the presents under it, we always had the real thing. But last year, Neil and I caught a whim to have a white tree.

Not a fake-snow-flocked white tree, but a genuine—and therefore artificial—white tree.

We weren't inspired by some fancy home-decorating magazine. We were just ready for something different. I thought it would be fun to decorate. A canvas of a different hue for family heirlooms. Neil dreamed of a clean-tree experience: no prickly branches, no needle droppings trailing from outside through the kitchen and piling up on the living room rug. No daily watering.

So we looked, but could not find one. The whim persisted, however, and this year we succeeded.

Instead of the annual trip to our favorite Christmas tree lot in North Haverhill, we marched into Rite Aid and came out with a long narrow box. No wind nipping at our noses, no cold feet as we tromped around seeking the perfect tree, no scent of pine and friendly conversation in the holiday spirit. Just a young clerk who fetched the box from out back and brought it to us.

A surreal tree-shopping experience.

At home, we began assembling it in the kitchen, fitting

together the stand and three sections. Its white "needles" began to shed as we put it together. They continued to drop as we carried it through the dining room into the living room, trailing white confetti.

Then we began the intricate process of unfolding and arranging the branches. Let me tell you, there are many, many branches—large and small—on an artificial tree. If you think natural tree branches are prickly, try the wire ends of the manufactured version. After my first session, I had scratches all the way up my forearms. And the "needles" continued to fall.

Unlike pine needles, which don't travel very far once they've dropped, the fake version gets charged with static electricity and leaps onto anything for a ride. Dog paws, cat paws, people feet—I swear they ride the thermals of the forced hot-air heat. I have little white strips from one end of the house to the other. I keep vacuuming, minus the pleasure of pine-freshened air cycling through the machine.

I'm sure it'll be quite lovely once I get it decorated. It's now a week after initial assembly and five days before Christmas; I'm still unfolding and arranging branches and branchettes in my spare time, armored in a long-sleeved sweatshirt.

Meanwhile, I've been thinking about tree farming—that sustainable, environmentally friendly North Country business. I feel badly that I've taken my annual contribution away from the industry. I think I'll buy a wreath to soothe my guilt.

The pine needles will be a pleasure.

library claus

Once upon a time, I told Peggy I had a hankering to try snowshoes. For years, I have missed walking in fields and forest during the winter.

Peggy is the librarian at the Baldwin Library in Wells River. She has chased down books for me from one end of New England to the other. She is a sterling member of that unsung-hero society of librarians.

But I digress. When I returned some books recently, Peggy said, "Didn't you say you wanted to try snowshoes?" With that, she produced a pair from behind her desk. I'm accustomed to librarians accomplishing assorted feats of magic, but this was a new one.

It turns out that The Freeman Foundation had offered grants to libraries and Peggy wrote a proposal for loaning "non-traditional" items. Ergo, the snowshoes. (Also, please note, fishing poles, a tent, and binoculars.)

I hadn't fulfilled my snowshoe yearning because I didn't want to buy before I could discover if I liked the activity and didn't know anyone who could loan me a pair. Life has taught me that lots of things are more fun in theory than in actuality.

Grabbing a walking stick, I took the shoes outside one sunny day.

I was tempted to put them on in the comfort of the sun-warmed enclosed front porch. A chilly wind blew and I didn't relish the notion of fussing with fastenings out there bare-handed. But even in my novice state, I realized walking down the front steps newly snowshoe-shod was a bad idea.

The steps were crusted with snow, so I couldn't sit down. Thus, I fumbled with the nylon straps in an awkward bent-over position, stretching muscles unaccustomed to the demand.

I finally got myself all strapped in and realized I hadn't brought my glasses outside. Forget it. The views would just be a bit fuzzy. Starting over was not an option.

What a thrill it was to walk on top of the snow over fields I've known for more than fifteen years.

When I got a good pace going, the soft thud of the shoes in the snow sounded like a heartbeat. Thump-thump, to a background symphony of the wind's ocean song through trees. When I came to a stop, I was embraced by that unique stillness of land hushed by deep snow.

With the sun shining on my face, I enjoyed expanded mountain views from a rise I couldn't have reached without snowshoes. My nearsightedness did not diminish the beauty.

Exhilarating—both the physical experience and the fulfillment of a long-held hankering. I waved gaily to occasional cars passing by, feeling very hardy-mountain-woman. All I lacked was the coonskin cap.

Snowshoeing is one of my best presents this holiday season. May you receive a pleasure equal to the gift my librarian gave me.

sighs of the season

'Tis the season to be jolly . . . or so they say.

But even if we pin jingling bells to our lapels and savor deep peace from the sacred joys of the season, the holidays are touched with bittersweet moments.

Here is one of the mysteries of joy: Even as we behold the grace of gifts, our hearts turn to longing. Gathered in celebration, surrounded by people we love, we are visited by thoughts of those no longer with us. It's impossible to participate in any ritual without thinking of other years, other times.

I cannot set my table without being assailed by memories. This soup tureen was my mother's. I take it from the cupboard and hear ringing echoes of her laughter. This ornament was my great-grandmother's. I know its story. My mother told me the tale as her mother told her, in a sentimental seasonal moment.

I have no children to tell it to, which seems especially sad as I decorate the tree with memories. Life takes the path it will. This is just one of the sighs of the season.

Christmas present is frosted by Christmases past.

There was a time when our tree stood tall, in the knotty-pine-paneled recreation room, laden with too much tinsel gleefully tossed by tiny hands. And I remember baking sheets of cookies I loaded with sugar sprinkles of red and green until they were nearly too sweet to eat. Colorful cards were strung across the mirror over the mantel; the crackling fire was scented with pine cones.

The delight of childhood Christmases was magic made by someone else. We were required only to look wide-eyed and rapturous, which took no effort.

The Christmas-morning rule in my childhood Virginia home was simple. My sister and I were not allowed to wake Mom and Dad until the streetlights went out in dawn's early glow. It makes me smile now to see us perched at the windowsill, willing the darkness to fade into sunrise.

My dad was a kid about Christmas. He'd sit by the tree, giving out presents one by one, so each could be savored and showcased. The year he had his first heart attack, he willed himself well enough to come home for Christmas Day, and returned to the intensive care unit the day after. But that day he was home, he was his familiar jolly holiday self. The doctors marveled. They didn't know Dad very well.

For me, the past is not a refuge from a threadbare present. There is much to gladden my holiday heart in this moment. But during these days when darkness turns toward the light of winter solstice, the shadows of days-gone-by play like dancers in the wings.

I am not uncomfortable with the sweet sadness.

Sorrow and smiles are entwined in holiday garlands. I am glad for the sadness, for tears sparkling like winter-bright stars.

Hark, the herald, memories sing.

snowlight

With the snow and slush and cold of recent weeks, it is easy to curse the season. Cars are coated with sheets of ice. A trip to the store is a treacherous trek. Plans must be flexible, unless one is willing to risk life and limb.

Flocks of finches have desperately descended on our feeders. It's so late for finches. Were they lulled by the unseasonable early-winter warmth and now cannot get south?

They are pretty, the finches, yellow or red. But they are contentious and scare away friendly chickadees. Nasty-tempered finches fight among themselves with frantic wings flapping, beaks flashing, and bitter territorial cries. Their bright colors bring me no pleasure.

The deep snow is crusted with ice. It breaks with small explosions under heavy boots. We cannot walk the dogs in the woods anymore. Small Teddy breaks through, then sinks into soft snow and cannot free himself for the next step. Crusty shards cut the pads of Devin's paws.

The kitchen is cluttered with scarves and hats and boots and gloves. The outside stairs invite accidents, and we'll need more wood before the season ends. Something large scurries behind the walls.

In the recent deep freeze, I nearly lost the skin off my fingers.

With hands still damp from a quick drying at the sink, I unlatched the metal hook on the back door. In an instant, the sub-zero temperatures froze the residual dampness on my skin. I pulled back fast enough to free my fingers, but felt that icy-sticky, stinging-numb feeling that brings to mind kids on a dare with tongues stuck to flagpoles.

It is easy to curse the season.

But one day I brave the cold to walk the dogs up the road in lightly falling snow at the tail end of a heavy storm. The hush is breathless. There is no way to describe the sacred silence of the countryside newly layered with snow. It makes you want to whisper.

And the air is piercing with freshness. It seems somehow new, with silken purity like a baby's skin.

But the most amazing effect comes as night falls. The moonless sky is blue velvet and the snow is bright in the darkness, glowing as if daylight is captured in the crystals. The mountains and trees are shadows in the distance, but the snow shines its eerie blue-white light.

It is a sight that stops me at the window. If mythical beasts and beings appeared, I would not be surprised. Snowlight creates a perfect setting for unicorns and their friends. I would not be surprised.

In snowlight, anything is possible.

In snowlight the curses of the season vanish, washed white to bliss . . . if only for moments.

It is enough.

ring-a-ding-ding

Just before New Year's, I broke my old rotary phone. In a clattering cataclysm, I knocked it off the shelf, sending it crashing to the uncarpeted wood floor. The housing cracked, broke away from the base, and a critical plastic piece was shattered where the line plugs in.

I pride myself on my tinkering abilities, but it was clear that rubber bands and adhesive tape would not put Humpty Dumpty together again. At least, not functionally.

In our home, it was the end of the era when phones *rang*.

Language is such an interesting thing. We still refer to phones ringing, though in truth they no longer ring at all. They beep. They buzz. They make annoying noises reminiscent of irritating alarm clocks.

Even after I surrendered to the siren song of a wireless phone that could accompany me around the house—house chores are more fun during long conversations with friends— I kept my old rotary phone for the simple pleasure of hearing it ring. Set at "loud," trilling chimes rose above the business-like summons of the push-button mobile phone.

When the transition from rotary phones began, offices and businesses were the first to switch. So the noise of the new phones was forever emblazoned on my aural consciousness as *official*, work-related—not a sound I wanted in my home.

And I liked dialing. (There's our quirky language again . . .

We still speak of *dialing* a number, though most of us have not had our fingers in the holes of that spinning wheel for years. Somewhere, a child is asking, "Mommy, why is it called dialing when I push buttons?") As the wheel went 'round, I'd collect my thoughts for the call I was making.

In those days, a real live person would always answer, or you'd get no answer at all. No machine pickups, no endless menu of choices recited by brainless, disembodied voices demanding that you choose a direction that never suits your needs.

Ah, it was a simpler time.

But mostly, I kept my old rotary phone not for the memories, but for the ringing.

What used to be the norm is now a specialty item. In fancy catalogs, I've seen advertisements for "nostalgic, old-fashioned rotary phones that ring!" You don't want to know what they cost.

Clearly, I am not the only one suffering with phone nostalgia.

My new phone's "ring" is less obnoxious than some. It is an electronic imitation of a ringing phone. It tries hard. Does its best. But like most imitations, it's really rather pathetic.

Bells have joyous associations that cannot be counterfeited. And as the cracked carcass of my old phone revealed, there actually was a bell in its innards. A graceful, shining, curved metal cup that sang of more relaxed times.

An era when there was time to ponder first words. When people answered, or when you simply waited until they could.

Farewell, phone. Your lighthearted ring is much missed.

buzz-z

One day last week, it was ten below zero. As I was feeding our wood furnace, I was bitten by a mosquito.

What's wrong with this picture?

How is it possible that mosquitoes thrive in a frosty, frozen world? Or is our basement an exclusive breeding ground?

Mosquitoes are the price I'm grudgingly forced to pay for summer-warm nights and fresh raspberries. But nowhere is it written in my North Country contract that amid the trials of winter I should also be searching for the AfterBite.

It's bad enough that cluster flies awake on days when the sun is strong enough to warm the windows. Combine cluster flies with cabin fever and it's nearly sent me running to the real estate agent.

Put the house on the market—I shall flee to a more hospitable (insectless) climate.

The January thaw moved in this week, complete with grimy snow and icy driveways. If I were really ambitious, I'd use this opportunity to finish last-minute fall chores that were buried under November snowdrifts. But I'm too busy battling flies and trying to figure out where those mosquito breeding grounds are hidden.

Now that temperatures have climbed to forty degrees, the biting creatures have fled, but I have a nasty suspicion they'll be back when it drops below zero again.

Meanwhile, this dreary January behaves more like mud season than winter. Dead gray skies complement foggy afternoons, and I keep wanting to adjust the contrast knob on the picture outside my windows.

Turning on more lights isn't an option. The power company has kicked in higher winter rates, and our electric bill has doubled. I'm left with the choice to live in the dark or brighten up and go broke.

I'll have to search for the mosquito breeding grounds by flashlight.

Andy Rooney did a bit on *60 Minutes* last week, disclosing that Vermont is among the five states that experience the least sunshine. Interestingly, New Hampshire was not listed in the sunless top five.

That does it for me.

I'm going to pack up my sunglasses, grab my beach blanket, and head down the hill into Woodsville to catch some rays.

get real

Are we as busy as we think we are, or does *thinking* about how busy we are just create more busy-ness?

I've been cogitating this concept for some time, which I totally blame on my farmer friends. Farmers make me philosophical.

Since moving to Ryegate Corner, I've had the pleasure of adding farmers to my inner circle and have observed a baffling phenomenon. While farmers are without doubt the busiest people I know, they are also the most unflappable.

Racking my memory to recollect a farmer in a tizzy, a rip-snorting, floor-stomping, self-pitying fit, I can't recall a one. Yet their routines are relentless.

Before dawn to after dark, day in day out, week after week, month after month. The frustrations of farming are high. Money is always an issue, machinery always breaks down, the weather always threatens, and the cows never go away.

Many local farmers carry the added emotional burden of trying to sustain multigenerational family farms. Theirs is a deep dedication to the land and to tradition. Despite their quiet ways, they are passionate about this way of life, a way of life beleaguered on all fronts.

Still, farmers are among the calmest, most uncomplaining people I know.

As if their own lives are not challenging enough, farmers

are often at the heart of their communities. They are volunteer firefighters, town clerks, church trustees, school board members, town librarians, and good neighbors.

I think I've learned their secret.

Farmers don't *expect* their work will ever be done. They don't *expect* things will run smoothly. They don't expect cooperation from nature, from machinery, from crops or cows. So what could be perceived as crises are considered common occurrences.

It is expectations that make us crazy.

Somewhere in the "oh, there's so much to be done" despair of busy-ness is the implication that there's an ideal end point. The notion that, given proper effort and circumstances, completion can be achieved.

Farmers don't labor under this illusion. They know better. Farmers don't think about being busy . . . they just put one foot in front of the other in a long-haul journey they know will involve obstacles every step of the way.

Lately, I've been cultivating the farmer frame of mind. Plodding along without idealized illusions. I'm setting out seeds, knowing the elements might not favor my efforts, no matter how conscientious I am. Tinkering with the gears of my to-do lists, shoveling the manure of interruptions and aggravations. And you know what?

I am less harried. I breathe more deeply. More gets done.

Life is hard and messy. So what else is new?

Let it be. Live with it.

Here is peace.

winter wild

The countryside is clothed in snow.

I cannot remember when so much snow stayed on the trees for so long. Wind or midday warmth usually strips the branches bare soon after snowfall.

Day after day, I awake to picture-postcard portraits of a classic New England winter. I reach for my camera and long for black-and-white film. So many luminous shades of white and gray in the early-morning light—color film cannot do it justice.

As I savor the view of the woods, I realize the snow-laden branches are like trees in full leaf. Gone are the skeletal frames through which I could see deep into the forest, into places hidden by fair-weather foliage. Branches blossom with snow; our crab apple tree is as lush as if it were in full bloom.

When the sun breaks through, the light is refracted in each twig's icy outline. Trees are filled with diamonds. The air sparkles with slivers of snow, like handfuls of glitter tossed on the breeze.

Such delicate beauty is so paradoxically heavy. Branches sag under the burden. Boughs break. The lilacs outside my sitting room window have shattered. Jagged, mortal wounds stand in a stark contrast to the surrounding soft white fluff. The chickadees, who usually perch in that tree to break open sunflower seeds, are unconcerned. They alight on broken branches we have not cleared away.

On a mercy mission, we trek to the remaining lilacs. We jostle bent and frozen branches, showering mini-blizzards down on ourselves. Gently. Feel the brittle wood, easily broken. Snow soft and light kisses my face, but snow amassed threatens the life of a tree.

In a state of winter contemplation, I stand at the kitchen sink watching plump mourning doves crowd the feeder. There is a crashing thump against the window. Reflexively I duck, frightened and confused. No small bird flying into the window could make such a racket. Behind me, Neil exclaims, "A falcon!"

We rush to peer over the sill, and there on our porch lies a magnificent bird. We hold our breath, hoping it is not badly injured. The head comes up, and we are pierced by the golden-eyed gaze of a wild predator.

I waste a few precious moments of this up-close encounter reaching for my camera. I barely have the bird in focus when it lifts off, gliding with broad-winged grace back into the woods.

Falcon or hawk? No birders we—despite this remarkably close encounter, we cannot distinguish between the two when we later consult our bird book.

It doesn't matter.

What remains in my memory is the fierce wildness of that eye, as if condemning us for the window . . . that wickedly curved beak . . . the rounded, luxuriantly feathered body and the joy of flight.

Uninjured it rose, soaring into the snow-softened woods, my spirit rising on its wings.

random acts of plowing

As if there weren't enough inconveniences imposed on us by winter, steady snowfall brings with it the perennial mystery of "when will the guy with the snowplow show up?"

Step right up, folks. It's that time of year when we are targets for random acts of plowing.

Don't get me wrong. A wonderful young fella plows our driveway and keeps the mailbox safe for the postal people. He generally shows up in a timely fashion; it's just that you never know what time that will be. Could be seven in the morning, seven at night, earlier or later. It just depends. His arrival can coincide with the morning shower, the day's first cup of caffeine, dinner, or a certain kind of private time better left unspecified in a column such as this.

All good citizens of the North know that, to get the greatest benefit from plowing, cars must be cleaned off, defrosted, and ready to pull out of the driveway. Plows prefer an open field for optimal play. It helps greatly if one is dressed, conscious and functional, ready to jump into boots and be off like a fireman when the alarm sounds.

Like everybody else I know with a plow on the front of his truck, our Rick is a workingman who picks up a little extra green by pushing the white around. Between one or two other jobs, I know Rick is out straight doing his best to take care of everyone on his route when the snow flies. And if he catches us at a bad time, he's real patient about letting us catch up to him.

I have no complaint with Rick. It's just the unpredictability of it all.

A friend of mine bought herself one of those snowblowers. She has rhapsodized about the joys of independence in driveway maintenance. When she wants it done, she just up and does it.

Our neighbor has one of those little plows that attaches to his riding mower. We often watch enviously as he clears his driveway whenever the spirit moves him.

We've thought about acquiring one of those rigs. But then, we think again. Between tending the furnaces (oil and wood), emptying the dehumidifier in the basement, refilling the humidifier upstairs, relighting the hot-water heater, walking the small dog who gets lost in drifts with the big dog who causes avalanches, feeding the birds, trying to get the fat cat to go out in weather she hates while trying to get the skinny cat to stop bouncing off the walls with cabin fever, I just can't face the maintenance factor of one more addition to our happy home—be it mechanical, feathered, or furred.

Thanks anyway. I'll stick with Rick.

So if you should see me out in the driveway some morning and catch a glimpse of nightgown below the hem of my coat, be kind.

I'm just the victim of another random act of plowing.

an enlightening tale

My friend Dee recently introduced me to bleach. Clorox-friendly women of my mother's generation may not understand why this is noteworthy—but baby boomers are afraid of bleach.

By the time I was old enough to take laundry seriously, I couldn't touch the stuff. It rots your clothes, don't you know. Eats holes through fabric any moth would envy. Kills elastic deader than foliage in winter. Makes colors run a marathon. Fearsome Bleach, the fascist of laundry products.

My first clue that maybe bleach wasn't so villainous came after we moved to our country home. Some hapless rodent found its way under the well cover and fell to a death by drowning. We only discovered this when our water took on a terrible stink. I got in the shower one morning and nearly passed out from the fumes.

I asked a native Vermonter about this puzzling phenomenon. He looked at me as if I didn't have the sense God gave little green apples and replied with a knowing snort, "Huh. Somethin' dead in yer well."

Solution? "Fish out the carcass and pour some bleach down 'er." The well, of course, not the carcass.

Bleach? In my well? My water supply? Surely you jest.

"That carcass will take a long time to decompose," he pointed out calmly.

Right. Neil fished and I poured.

I poured far too much. Turned my hair nearly a shade lighter and, boy, were my fingernails white. We drank bottled water until it flushed through, but the sinks and tubs were really clean.

Even then, it didn't occur to me to use the stuff on my clothes. Then my mother died, and, as years passed, the pristine linen tablecloths I'd lovingly brought back from my dismantled California home were dotted with stains and had begun to gray.

Looking at them made me sad. It was an affront to my mother. My childhood memories are replete with visions of those same tablecloths, snowy white on her well-laid tables.

"Bleach," Dee said.

"I can't," I wailed in horror. "They're old. They'll rot and fall apart."

"Nonsense," Dee sniffed. "Nothing but bad press. I use bleach on nearly everything. Have for years. Never harmed a thing. You just have to use it right."

So I've been learning how to use it right. And this holiday season, when I laid Mother's good dishes on her once-again-snowy-white linen, I got to thinking.

I wonder how many other things I've needlessly feared.

Caution is a good thing. But so is the courage to change your perceptions, and common sense conquers a lot of foolishness.

It doesn't take two cups of bleach to purify the well.

Thanks, Dee.

burning the torch

Thousands of miles from the Salt Lake City Olympics, I cry out "Oh, *no!*" when Evgeni Plushenko falls out of his quadruple toe loop.

A mogul skier drops from a jump into a hole, lands with his knee folded sideways, tumbles down the hill, and rises with his face contorted in pain. I groan.

American snowboarders—those radical, stoked, Gen-X renegades of sport—stand on the podium in a historic medals sweep. Not since 1956 have Americans taken gold, silver, and bronze in a single event. As our national anthem plays, the super-cool young men's eyes fill with tears. Ross Powers, Danny Kass, and Jarret Thomas are unashamed of their emotions.

I watch sports I know little or nothing about and hold my breath. I root for athletes whose names I've never heard, sometimes from countries I'd be hard-pressed to find on a map.

Why? What is this Olympic compulsion?

For me, it's about the stories, and every Olympian has one. Every story has common threads—passion, dedication, discipline. But every story is also unique.

Speed skater Casey FitzRandolph comes back from difficulties to win gold. In the stands, his legally blind grandfather savors his triumph, with the aid of special glasses. I don't know who to be happier for, Casey or Granddad.

After a two-year, soul-searching break, Todd Eldredge decided to go to Salt Lake City. The former world figure-skating champion has held the U.S. title six times, but he has returned empty-handed from previous Olympic quests. "I wouldn't feel right about myself if I didn't try it one more time," he said. He is thirty years old.

Former skater Scott Hamilton said that learning a quadruple toe loop at Eldredge's age is like learning a new language. But Eldredge learns it, has the courage to go for it—and misses. His impressive career will not be capped with Olympic honors.

And yet, at the end of his routine, knowing his dream is forever lost, Todd's face seems to reflect peace. I like to think that was the moment when he found fulfillment in his final effort.

As Eldredge waits for what will surely be painful scores, a young fan's voice rings out.

"You're a great champion, Todd." A poignant moment of pure truth.

What awes me is not merely the winning of medals. What engages me isn't the treasure of gold, silver, and bronze. It's knowing that every athlete has a story, and every story is one of sacrifice, courage, passion, determination, commitment, and power.

I am aware that I watch a lifetime of effort condensed into minutes or seconds of make-or-break performance. That parents have woken up in the wee hours to drive their kids to the rink. That towns have held bake sales to help one of their own pursue the Olympic dream.

It is cliché to say every athlete is a winner, medals or not. To me, it's more than that.

They embody something heroic in the human spirit, and standing witness uplifts me.

woods truth
and tree wisdom

It was one of those steel-gray February days. Laboring in fields domestic, I picked up, swept up, cleared up, and cleaned up until I was fed up.

Tossing aside rags and rancor, I fled to the uninviting outdoors. Though dim and drear, it at least offered the charms of nothing to sort, straighten, or shine. Deadfall in the woods may rest where it drops.

The dogs were delighted with the unexpected boon of a midday romp. I very nearly couldn't lace up my boots for their dancing joy at my feet.

I grab my walking stick—an inelegant, unvarnished staff stripped of bark by time and the elements. The hard-packed snow of midwinter is uneven and icy. More than a year after a trauma, I am still careful of my injured knee. The staff is not affectation but a necessity.

Outside, the dogs bound ahead and double back to me, as if demanding that I share their high spirits. I am not cheered. I am a refugee fleeing domestic oppression.

But as I walk, the cold, clean air calms me. Though the brook is mostly silent, it burbles beneath the ice. It murmurs under the frozen landscape, vibrant life gathering force for the explosion of spring.

A trick of the light illuminates the landscape in hues of a fine black-and-white photograph. I have seen this effect before, but no matter. It stops me in my tracks every time.

I have come nearly full circle in the woods, to the Grandmother Tree. An ancient maple, gnarled and wounded by lightning, she is majestic still. A magnificent living force of nature. Lay your hands on her weathered trunk and it is easy to believe she whispers secrets drawn deep from the dark of earth . . . if only I knew the language.

Standing there, chilled and thrilled in the strange light, I am quieted. One small human bundled against the cold, in a landscape grand and untamable by mop or broom.

The thought passes through my mind that this is how we were for longer than we have lived in houses. Nomads on the land, creatures like any other, subject to the whims of nature and fully aware of our small place in the wild.

I look back through the trees toward the house. It is small against the sweep of woods and hill and valley. The rooms within, with all their clutter and claptrap, are insignificant from my vantage point under the outspread arms of the Grandmother Tree.

We spend too much time indoors.

We forget who we are in piles of papers, ringing phones, and beguiling electronic wizardry. We begin to believe we are the pivot point on which the world turns, with our to-do lists, dates, and deadlines.

We begin to believe in our own importance.

Grandmother Tree knows better.

country quiet

Some of us do not greet the day with perky enthusiasm. We come to consciousness in stages, and woe betide anyone who interferes with this process.

What I want in the morning is a cup of tea and lots of silence.

I might read. Sometimes I meander through shadowy corridors of reverie, chasing a piece of a dream or an elusive thought—renegade images I later tease into a column or poem.

As I get older, my hunger for this waking quiet time becomes more intense. Fifteen minutes used to be enough to give my day a good start. That became a half hour, then an hour. Now I like to have nearly two hours to get the engines up and running.

Some people would say I'm slowing down. I prefer to think of it as leisurely wisdom. In my younger days, I'd leap out of bed, into the shower, gulp down some tea, and be on the road to work before I was fully awake. My leaping days are gone.

Good riddance.

One morning, I was cocooned in quietude when the dogs suddenly went berserk.

Anyone who has dogs knows they "speak" in different tones, just like people. There's the "Oh, goodie, Neil's home," announcement when his car pulls into the driveway. My dogs love company, so guests are greeted with the "Visitors!!" delight.

When other dogs wander into sight, the "Intruder, intruder!" alarm sounds. But most raucous is the big-animal frenzy. The sight of cows or horses sends them into snarling, snapping, growling, howling hysterics. Given where we live, this is not an uncommon occurrence.

Usually, we have some warning before this madness is unleashed. The clip-clop of horse hooves, a glimpse of some-one walking a cow down the road.

When my quiet time was shattered on this day, the doggy cacophony exploded without any hint and exceeded the big-animal fury. To say I was startled would be a monumen-tal understatement. My heart rate accelerated, adrenaline charged through my veins. Alarmed, I ran to the porch.

I looked out into the yard, and what a sight greeted me.

High in the crab apple tree, incongruous and ungainly among the small branches, were three wild turkeys pecking at the shriveled remains of crab apples. As they fed, they would lose their balance and fall out of the tree. In awkward tur-key flight, they would rise again, sometimes crashing into one another on the way up, on the way down, or both.

It was an avian Three Stooges show.

There was no point in trying to settle the dogs down. We three watched those three, the snarling, screaming dogs set-ting a musical score to flailing wings and turkey-corpulent dance. Inside the enclosed front porch, dog noise bounced and reverberated, accompanied by my helpless laughter.

Those who sing the praises of the quiet country life rarely live in the country.

town meeting tapestry

Before I moved to the North Country, "Town Meeting" was a quaint notion, something I had only read about or seen in old movies.

But since moving here, I've never missed the annual event. I was a teacher, and school was closed for the special day. It just didn't seem kosher not to go.

It only took once. I was hooked.

I discovered there is nothing quaint about Town Meeting. Sometimes contentious, sometimes routine, but always entertaining, this gathering reveals the invisible threads that weave the tapestry of community.

What is said is often less important than who says it.

Unwritten rules govern Town Meeting. Rules as binding as the parliamentary procedure so deftly managed by town moderators. I was instructed in these critical rules by Pat Rhoads, a longtime resident of Newbury, where I saw my first eleven years of local democracy in action.

"Listen, learn, *and don't say a word*," she sternly admonished.

Townfolk take a dim view of newcomers taking the floor.

She explained that three years was a good minimum residency requirement to consider before going beyond joining the chorus of "aye" or "nay" at the appropriate time. And even after that, she instructed, if you *must* speak, do not speak more than once.

At Town Meeting, them that speaks the least is listened to the most.

Those who know me well will have no difficulty imagining what a challenge this posed. Pat nearly dislocated my shoulder yanking me down each time I was possessed by the impulse to rise and speak. Had she not done so, I would have made those newcomer mistakes that seal one's doom for years to come.

I recently met someone who moved to Vermont ten years ago and did not have the benefit of a Pat to show him the way. He told me he'd stood up at Town Meeting from the first, taking on the town's hottest issues.

"You *didn't*," I breathed in horror.

"I didn't know any better," he said mournfully. "And once I learned, it was too late. Branded a troublemaking, pushy flatlander.

"I haven't said a word at Town Meeting in five years," he went on sadly. "But it doesn't matter. If I'm going to get a fresh start, I'll have to move to another town. Far away."

This year after the meeting, I spoke with a man who'd made a motion I felt was really important. In the twelve years I've lived in Ryegate, I've heard him speak less than half a dozen times.

"Well," he said with a worried grin, "later I really wanted to bring up this other point, but I was afraid that'd be too much."

His family has lived in town for seven generations.

Whoever said small-town life is simple has never lived in one. Not in the North Country, anyway.

a song for the unsung

Each year at Town Meeting time, I'm struck anew by how many of my neighbors tend to our community's business. Their unheralded efforts fill the pages of the Town Report.

Turn to the list of town officers. From the high-profile town moderator to the rarely glimpsed cemetery commissioners, folks quietly take care of business year-round. Their responsibilities involve tidal waves of paperwork, eons of meetings and thankless tasks that would give Job a significant challenge.

Most of what they do could only be truly appreciated if they ceased doing it.

If paid at all, their remuneration is a pittance given the hours, effort and aggravation involved. On the rare occasions when their work is acknowledged, it's often on the firing line of complaint. Yet year after year, many positions are held by the same people, some of whom wear multiple hats in the parade of town government.

Were it not for them, ballots would languish uncounted, libraries would be bookless, weeds would obscure ancestors' graves, and things would generally be in a nasty tangle.

But there's more. Not listed on the town officials' page are others who labor on our behalf. Consider volunteer firefighters and their inexplicable willingness to have their lives disrupted at all hours. Day or night, at twenty below or hotly humid, firefighters dash out the door to face very real dangers.

Despite their selflessness, odds are that the next day someone will gripe. No matter how quickly firefighters arrived at the scene, no matter how much (or whom) they managed to save, someone will say they shoulda been there quicker and done better.

Then there are unlisted people like Dale Wright of Ryegate. Every year for fifteen years, Mr. Wright has driven one hundred miles in two days, hand-delivering some three hundred Town Reports. It's hard to believe Ryegate even has that many miles of road, but Mr. Wright should know, having driven them in ice and mud and snow.

Now seventy years old, Mr. Wright was seeing ahead to a time when he might not be able to continue his appointed rounds. He suggested that the town could use his pay in another way. But many Ryegate residents weren't happy with the impersonal alternatives of mailing or leaving reports at key locations for pickup. "I don't know," my friend Holly said after Town Meeting, "those options just don't seem . . . Well, they just aren't *Ryegate*."

Mr. Wright has left a legacy with his annual quick knock on the door and ten seconds of friendly chat. Now many of us don't want to settle for less.

All these people who labor on our behalf define the character of our community. Their efforts shape who we are and what kind of town we live in.

From listers to delinquent-tax collectors, to all the folks who do those jobs, I say thank you.

— spring —

frosting spring

H ere in the North Country, nature clothes herself in weather excesses like a fashion fiend with no spending limit. If you prefer climatic moderation, this is not the place to live.

Fall is an explosion of glory. Winter is deep and cold. Spring is often a poignant sprint into summer. Summer compensates for its brevity with the drama of thunderstorms, heat waves, and dripping humidity.

I sometimes wonder about the relationship between weather and regional character. Are Southerners languid, right down to the drawl in their speech, because of their long, hot summers? Do Californians compensate for the lack of seasonal variety with personal flamboyance and eccentricities?

Is North Country reticence and understatement a no-frills-necessary response to a climate where nature always puts on a show?

I ponder such things on the first day of spring, gazing out at a countryside freshly frosted in white.

Prior to the latest snowfall, we were mired in mud season—the time that tries the soul. Mucky roads, days of dreary skies, stark landscapes awaiting spring's greening touch. A friend of mine, a kindred spirit who suffers with mud season morbidity, described the view from his windows as a deathly specter.

"The trees," he lamented, "look like skeletons scrabbling desperately toward the heavens in some vain hope of salvation."

Though I had little cheer to share, I tried to lift his spirits with early observations of renewal. One sunny day, I told him, I'd driven to Hanover and seen crocuses blooming by a friend's doorway. (I left out the part about three grown women crouching on the ground by the delicate buds, breathing in careful unison as if our very presence might fracture the fragile evidence of spring.)

But he could not be cheered.

"It's worse than an Alfred Hitchcock movie set out there," he said.

I know just how he feels. Which is why, despite my own desperate longing for leaves, I have not been unhappy with this new-fallen snow. It is a relief from the brown, brown, brown. A merciful mud season masquerade, covering dead grasses and outlining skeletal branches in fluffy finery.

The banks of the brook wear ruffles of ice. Rain and melting snow raised the water level. As it dropped again, freezing temperatures edged the banks in lacy adornment.

This touch of winter has a frivolous feeling. I know it won't last long. It's a playful fling of a mischievous spring, relieving the drag of mud season. I'm grateful.

I remember a year when leaves didn't pop out until early June. I nearly lost my mind. It could be a long brown journey into green—I welcome a little white to lighten my way.

So I settle back in this North Country theater and watch the show. Trying to enjoy each act, not rushing ahead in anticipation of the seasonal shift I long for. Cultivating patience— these are the first seeds I plant for spring.

Awaiting the harvest of green.

wild water and crazy cats

It is the season of dirty snow, naked earth, and patches of sodden dead leaves, sucking mud-rutted roads, skeletal trees whipping piteously under lashes of wind-driven sleet.

It is the season of madness.

The grace of winter has fled, taking with it the cathedral hush of a snow-blanketed world. In its place, sand-littered roads grate under tires. Following other cars is often a dangerous skirmish with pebble-missiles fired into windshields.

A friend who lives farther south tells me the crocuses are in bloom, but I can't relate to that. Like the possibility of water on the moon, it is a distant concept with no reality here in the world where I live.

February spoiled us with record-setting sunshine; now March extracts payback with leaden skies, icy rain, and occasional hints of spring that North Country folk know better than to believe in.

Frozen in silence for so long, our backyard brook rushes in rain-swollen tumult, making its own wild dash to spring. But midstream, the rocks are still sheeted with ice.

The cats are crazed. Nature on the edge of spring confounds them. Lulled by warm sunshine occasionally beaming through windows, they expect welcoming warmth outdoors. But brief forays on paw-numbing packed snow leave them disgruntled, and in they want to come.

They return, flicking quick tongues over muddy paws and cold-nipped ear tips, growling their displeasure at me as if I am responsible for this nonsense.

"It's not my fault," I grumble back.

"Yeah, right," their disgusted looks reply.

Five minutes later, they want out again, as if the season might have changed from one moment to the next.

Is it spring yet?

Had I earned a nickel for each time I let out or let in one or both cats on a particularly maddening March day, I would have a small fortune. Instead, reviewing my accomplishments at day's end, I can recall nothing but serving the door-tending demands of my imperious felines.

The sap of spring rises in furry breasts. Denied outdoor play, our cats and dogs transform the house into an arena for games of tag. They lie in wait, pounce, dash upstairs, careen around corners, thunder downstairs, leap and roll, and perform every feat short of bouncing off the walls.

There is little joy in their games. Their cavorting is edged with desperation.

I am empathetic.

As snowmelt seeps into my basement laundry room, I tiptoe past puddles to the washing machine. Solid ground is but a dream in my dooryard. The house feels colder than in the heart of winter. Lucky souls take flight for destinations where warmth is more than an illusion, while I gaze at distant snow-capped mountains illuminated in frigid sunlight.

And, like my cats, I sit by the door waiting for spring.

endless winter

When this column appears, I bet the snow will still be up to our windowsills.

A few weeks ago, we asked Jeremy to come over with his backhoe. If we didn't clear away the snow banked against the house, we'd need a rowboat for our basement laundry room when those mountains melted.

The nice thing about metal roofs is that the snow slides off rather than staying put. Loaded snow on shingled roofs cyclically melts and freezes, causing ice dams and interior water damage. The not-so-nice thing about metal roofs is that avalanches of snow cuddle up to the house.

Thanks to the last two storms that blew through, you'd never know Jeremy had already hauled and shoved away a season's worth of snow. I console myself with the thought that if he hadn't, we couldn't glimpse even a patch of sky out our windows.

While clutched in winter's stubborn snow-blown grip, I've amused myself by observing that the most die-hard, dyed-in-the-wool, native North Country residents have reached the end of their winter tolerance.

Complaining about winter to these folks usually gets you a laconic rebuke, delivered in a rapidly disappearing regional drawl. "Way-uhl, it's wintah and this *is* Verrr-mont." Ringing through this statement are tones that clearly say, "What did you expect, you down-country fool?"

So forgive me if, after decades of being put in my place, I take delight in hearing these folks mutter their own grumble or two.

I'm strangely strengthened by these cracks in the granite of native North Country temperament. My own endless-winter doldrums seem validated. I feel less like a winter-wimp when even the crustiest old-timers aren't dismissing this season with a "Way-uhl, it's nothin' like the wintah of . . ." Instead, they are saying, "Reminds me of those wintahs when I was a kid."

This may seem like a subtle concession. But live long enough in the North Country and you come to appreciate such finer points. If this winter lives up to winters past, baby, it's baaad.

Although everyone I've talked to is hungry for green by now, their hankering is tempered by the prospect of mud season and spring cleanup. When all this snow melts, it's going to be a mess. Broken branches and other winter wreckage lurk under the drifts.

It'll be some long while before we get to laze in warm sunshine.

I look out at the dog yard that runs along the side of our barn. The fence has been assaulted and is partially collapsed from loads of snow careening off the roof. That'll be one of our first jobs when we can reach it. Out another window, I look on a mangled lilac that will need a chain-saw rescue.

Wherever I look, work waits for snowmelt. Still, I'm ready to make that trade for the green of spring.

a bedtime story

At night, before sleep, I like to read for a while. But at this time of year, that's nearly impossible.

The flies won't let me.

I crawl into bed with my book, turn on the light, and they come. Drawn by the warmth of the lamp, they sneak out of devilish hiding places to converge on the ceiling and walls above. Buzzing and beating their foul bodies against the ceiling in mad ecstasy, the flies destroy the quiet I treasure before folding into sleep.

I keep a clean house. There is no rotting matter on which they can feast. But still they come, the first and ugliest precursors of spring. Big flies, little flies. Fat, furry flies. One by one they come, until at least a dozen of the nasty things are feeding on the light, dotting the ceiling above my head.

In frustration, I put the book down and turn off the lamp.

I feel them there, in the darkness. Humming with spastic movement, the flies take time to settle. Even then, I feel their presence. And there is always one, the fattest, that continues to bounce against the ceiling with frenetic insistence long after the others have given up.

After this most persistent beast has come to rest, I am still uneasy. I lay quiet, senses alert. Worrying that they might fall dead in the night on my bed, on my head . . . perhaps even into my mouth, gone slack with sleep.

It is an Alfred Hitchcock moment. They are there. The ordinary turned malevolent. *The Birds* in miniature. Determined to reclaim the night, one evening I took the vacuum upstairs and did battle before bed. I stalked and hunted down every fly, feeling grim satisfaction as each one was sucked into the bowels of the machine. It was not an easy task.

Have you ever chased a dancing fly with the small opening of a vacuum hose?

But when the duel was done, when even the window casements were clear, the room was fly-free. I closed the door, so the rear guard could not advance.

Silence.

With a sigh, I crawled into bed with my book. I turned on the bedside lamp. Savored the quiet and began to read.

You know what happened next. One by one . . .

Old houses have many secrets but nighttime readers are persistent people. I borrowed a trick from childhood, nearly forgotten until need arose . . .

These nights, you'll find me under the covers, reading by flashlight.

the garbage man

Walter Wilcox has been picking up our trash ever since we moved to Ryegate Corner more than ten years ago. In rain, sleet, hail, snow, or heat, Walter pulls up in his truck every Wednesday, gets out of the cab, bends over, picks up the heavy bags, and hurls them high on top of the pile already heaped in the back.

Once a month, Walter walks to the porch and sets the bill inside. If there's a car in the driveway, he takes a shortcut and lays the handwritten bill on the driver's seat.

There are few things in life as reliable as Walter. The sun rises and sets each day, and on Wednesday Walter picks up our garbage. So this past week, when his appointed time came and went and the bags still sat at the end of the driveway, we worried about Walter.

It's true that it had been snowing for two days and was bitter cold. The excellent Ryegate road crews were doing their usual best to keep on top of things, but high winds and blowing snow conspired against them. That Wednesday morning, I took one look at the white ribbon of road and decided to work at home instead of risking a wretched slide down into town. But still, I worried about Walter. Snow had never stopped him before.

That evening, Neil brought the bags back in, and I called Walter. I left a message on his machine, even more concerned by the long tone indicating that others had been calling him, too.

A few hours later, Walter called back. In his North Country drawl, as always peppered with an assortment of mild swear words, he admitted to setting out that morning and turning back.

"The wind was blowin' so much snow I couldn't see a ***damn thing," he said with disgust. "An' I had a wake to get to later on. I was afraid I'd get up in them Ryegate hills and get myself stuck somewheres. So I said to hell with it and came on home."

I tendered my sympathies on the death in his family and assured him it wasn't our trash I'd worried about—it was him.

"Naw," he said, "I'm all right. 'Course I've had this damn noo-moan-ya," he added angrily. "An' there's this broken collarbone they found when they did them X-rays. Don' know where that come from. Don' remember ever breakin' it.

"I dunno," he went on. "Ever since my last birthday it just seems like it's been one ***damn thing after another. I'm gettin' along, you know. I'm thinkin' maybe it's time for me to quit. Gettin' to be an ole man."

Walter is eighty-four. I laughed and said he'd been an old man when he first started picking up for us.

"Naw," he scoffed, "I was only sev'nty-five."

There's something to be learned from people like Walter, but I'll be ***damned if it can be put into words.

My favorite Walter-wisdom comes from running into him one day in town. I asked how life was treating him.

"Life always treats me just fine," he replied that day. "It's the people in it that'll make you crazy."

Now, there's a distinction worth chewin' on.

shadows of spring

Under steel-gray skies—a specialty of dreary mud season—we take to the woods. The trees are bare. Not even a hint of buds. Spring fades to a faint hope in the heart.

The skeletal maples have become so familiar in their stripped-down hibernation, it's difficult to believe they will ever be dressed again in deciduous glory.

Patches of snow hide in forest shadows. The dogs find them with glee, tracking their frosty surfaces with muddy paws—blissfully rolling in squirming, leg-flailing delight.

I think sometimes that this is the dogs' favorite time of year. They run across open ground, no undergrowth tugging at their fur, the spongy forest floor soft under their paws, scents of woods creatures strong on exposed earth. Yet there is still snow to play in.

The dogs snuffle along in an olfactory orgy, darting from one invisible trail to another, pawing at small burrows. They thrust their muzzles into little openings in minor acts of destruction . . . undoing the efforts of some night critter that had dug itself into the pine-needled forest floor.

Moving deeper into the woods, we come across green and flattened ferns, startlingly verdant against the brown, decomposing humus under the trees. They are perfectly formed and vibrant, emerald enchantments on the ground. No other new growth pierces the still-sleeping earth, yet here are these fully grown ferns.

Had they slept, cryogenically preserved under winter snows, now revived? Or, if newly grown, why are they flattened against the ground?

Someone with more woods knowledge than I may have the answers. I prefer the mystery. We caress the fresh fronds with wondering fingertips. In weeks to come, there will be a riot of green, and each fern will not seem so precious.

The woods' history is revealed in the starkness of pre-spring. In some century past, these acres were orchards and fields. Where rock walls once stood, scattered stones gather, half sunk into the ground in ragged rows. Naked of underbrush, they are testaments to some farmer's labors, stone by stone evoking the sweat of his brow.

What would he think, I wonder, of this land that abides but is not worked? Would he think it a waste? Or be grateful that at least there is no paving here?

Ferns and stones and snow traces captivate us, but it is the brook that fascinates. While the others just hint at spring, the stream carries the message with boisterous vigor. Snowmelt and rain have transformed quiet waters into a rushing furor, swift and strong, white-watering over rocks like little Niagaras.

Under leaden skies, I gaze into the water where it eddies in pools below the falls. No reflections dance on its surface. I see dark waters bright and clear.

Dark waters bright and clear, with spring still a breath away.

spring cleaning (sort of)

It's that time of year. Time to throw open the closets, to refresh and renew dark places where clutter has hibernated through winter.

The onset of warm sunshine and balmy breezes inspires a hunger to clean house. Perhaps we want our homes to be as fresh as the air we gulp like heady champagne when we dash around triumphantly opening windows.

But even with such inspired motivation, thinning out my wardrobe always slows me down. Why are old clothes so difficult to let go? They might be tattered at the edges, woefully outdated or too snug for comfort, but year after year I re-file some clothes like old love letters that cannot be thrown away.

I once read a *New York Times* column on this subject. The author pointed out that certain items of clothing become symbols of stages in our lives, or reflect elements of our personalities we do not want to lose.

Right on, I thought, considering the dashiki-print caftan hanging next to my sensible North Country turtleneck tops. Newly graduated from high school, I wore that caftan in the heady days of first freedom from the parental abode.

It was 1969. The place was San Francisco. I hung out in coffeehouses, dreaming of being a poet.

No matter that the hem unraveled long ago, or that it's too

tight across my back. Having it in my closet reminds me of idealistic days and the pristine belief in a writer's dreams.

The tee shirt from my high school boys' gymnastics team takes up scarce drawer space. In those pre–Title 9 days, girls' teams didn't rate their own uniforms. Boys got a new tee each season. Our challenge was to convince one of the guys to give up his. Not an easy task. Many a short-lived gymnast-romance came under suspicion of tee-shirt intent.

I won mine not through romance, but through the kindness of a graduating senior. Rick was a ring man, built like a V. He was quiet and gentle and had the same girlfriend all through high school. She was as quiet as he. Rick gave me his tee shirt because he knew how much it meant. It was his comment on the injustice of girls not having their own.

It is as thin and soft as fine fabric now. But the coveted SKYLINE GYMNASTICS is still bright red. I've hand-stitched disintegrating seams innumerable times. I wear it rarely to preserve its life, but I know that even if it were reduced to shreds, I could not let it go.

It is a reminder of an era of heart-thumping competitive excitement, and of a time when the sting of inequality was softened by a boy who understood.

So though I clean and clear, my closets and drawers will always be more cluttered than they could be.

This is a price I'm willing to pay . . . for reminders that enrich my life, for memories that make me smile.

winter state of mind

We're on the brink of spring. Stuck in the mud, surrounded by brown—but I spied buds on our lilac tree yesterday. In my garden, daylilies have sent green shoots scouting above the ground.

The brook is hale and hearty, rushing over rocks as if delirious with freedom. While I was changing the sheets in the upstairs bedroom, two Canada geese flew by the window. Fat and sassy they were, and close enough that I could marvel at their detailed markings as they winged gracefully northward.

We have had days when the morning sun was strong enough to heat our enclosed front porch. Strong enough that we could open the kitchen door and let the balmy solar-warmed air into the house.

Yet, I find, it isn't easy to let go of the winter state of mind.

We cocoon in winter. Like hibernating animals, we take sanctuary in our caves. We seek home and hearth against the furies of raw wind and snow. The quietude of the sleeping, white-blanketed world outside seeps into our spirits. We shift into low gear, conserving energy.

As winter loosens its icy grip, I emerge gradually from my cave. Slowly, like the inch-by-inch emergence of new green in my garden. As if caution is called for. Not quite trusting that another storm won't swoop down and lay its icy mantle on my head.

Snow scrapers and brushes are still on the floor of my car. Headed outside, I grab my winter coat, hat, and gloves as a matter of course. On some days, thus bundled, I sit sweating behind the wheel and realize a lighter coat would have sufficed.

The unconscious anticipation of dangerous, unpredictable road conditions is still keen. I make appointments and plans with icy roads in mind. These days, however, the worst I'm likely to encounter is rain.

Some afternoons, when the sun shines, I'm taken by surprise—discovering that it's nice enough to sit on the open back porch. The heat is captured under the roof, and if the wind doesn't blow down from the north, I can turn my face to the sun, close my eyes, and feel warmth stealing into my bones.

But when the wind picks up, it is a strange sun-warm, air-cold experience. This time of year presents such contrasts. The crocuses may be blooming, but there is snow in our woods, pockets where the chill still reigns.

We dance these days between winter and spring. What will it be today? The slow waltz of winter subsiding, or a sprightly spring fox-trot?

Do I need the heavy coat, or will a jacket do? Is it warm enough to open the doors, or is the wind raw-edged with winter's trailing touch?

These questions mark the way out of winter state of mind, as I unfurl from the cocoon where I have cuddled against the cold.

name game

What's in a name? Possibly, reduced repair bills. Give a machine a name and it reacts with gratitude, delivering a better performance in return. Or so we hope.

Laugh if you will. But consider this. In World War II, pilots named the planes that carried them into battle. The choice was a significant, symbolic business.

It's not enough for us that a collection of mechanical parts merely does its job. There is a human impulse to create identity for the inanimate equipment we rely on. The impulse to create a relationship.

If you snicker at the notion of naming your automobile, I ask you this . . . Do you get into your car on a cold winter morning and, before turning the ignition key, mutter "C'mon, baby," or some such encouragement?

And once the car has obligingly started, do you pat the dashboard gratefully with a silent or spoken, "That's a good girl"?

If you're going to talk to it, you might as well give it a name. The principle remains the same.

Many people might not confess to conversing with their cars. I am not among them. As a result, I had an interesting exchange with a local mechanic. I shall not reveal his identity. The man has a business to run, and the general public may not consider his attitude as enlightened as I do.

Dropping my car off for a tune-up, I gave the hood a gentle

slap and said, "Don't worry, girl, they'll take good care of you." I'm accustomed to talking to my car in private but had forgotten the mechanic was standing there.

Caught in the act, I blushed. I considered making a joke out of my car conversation, but the words never made it to my lips. There he stood, the rugged North Country mechanic, smiling at me. Shrugging, I grinned. "Yep, I talk to my car."

"Good thing," he replied calmly.

"Excuse me?" I said, surprised.

"A-yuh. A good thing," he said.

"Why's that," I asked.

Wiping his hardy hands on a rag, he said, "Cars that get talked to run better."

"Really?" said I, shocked not by his statement, but by his willingness to utter it.

"Yup. Don't understand it. Just know it's true."

I got to thinking about this the other day. If it works for cars, why not for other essential machines?

Let me introduce you to our furnace. Her name is Gertrude.

It wasn't until years after this column appeared that I learned protecting the identity of my car mechanic was unnecessary. Tim Spooner, owner of Groton Garage, stands behind his experience.

"I think it's funny," he laughed.

magical, musical memory

I s there some special part of the brain devoted to storing song lyrics?

Amid all the knowledge in our gray matter, isn't it amazing that tucked away somewhere are all the words to "Harper Valley PTA"?

And why?

I genuinely love learning and have a high regard for history. Then why do all the lyrics of "Monster Mash" spring forth at the opening chords, but I can't recite more than the first few lines of Lincoln's "Gettysburg Address"?

What is it about music that so imprints words in our memories that we remember commercial jingles from childhood, but our parents' anniversaries always take us by surprise?

As if lyrical memory itself were not enough, few songs come back to us without a wealth of associated sensory details from long ago. The Beatles' "We Can Work It Out" brings back sights and scents from my first dances and first love.

The smooth–rough texture of his corduroy jacket, the blue crepe paper hanging in the gym, that cologne I would recognize even if I were standing in a field freshly spread with manure. The feel of his slightly sweaty hand in mine. My nervousness, wondering if he would kiss me right there in front of God, everybody, and the chaperones.

That's a lot of baggage for a few notes to carry.

Each generation has its own music, its own memories. Sinatra's "Me and My Gal" takes me back to a California kitchen where my parents danced, singing along to "their song." My mother, a tall woman, bent over with her head on Dad's shoulder. An awkward height combination, but no less graceful for the discrepancy. They danced, caught in their own memories of early love, creating memories for me. They are dead now, but many songs bring them back—my mother's trilling laugh, my father's crooked grin.

It was Dad who introduced me to the blues, sitting cross-legged on the living room floor in front of the console stereo he called "the Victrola." As the wailing tones of music came through the speakers, he told me the sad tale of Billie Holliday's life, the trials of Miles Davis, stories of racism that drove so many black musicians to Europe. And when Dad died, the most precious gift I brought home was his record collection.

Every groove is an unbroken line of my history.

And though the twenty-something clerk looked at me oddly when I insisted my first CD stereo system be equipped with an antiquated turntable, I was not embarrassed. Those revolving platters carve my paths into the past, where the long-dead still dance and tell the stories, which have now become mine.

Where the magic of musical memory enchants me still, and always will.

here comes the sun

The gloomy month of April has made this year's passage from winter to spring a journey of mythic proportions. Day after day, week after week, dreary overcast skies have tried the souls of the most hardy North Countryites.

Even taciturn and stolid old-timers have been heard to mumble edgy, disconsolate commentaries in this dark time. Faced with slowly emerging shoots of green in my garden, I have barely restrained myself from speeding their growth with desperate tugs.

Now there is one, *one*, sprightly bunch of daffodils finally blossoming in my yard—in a spot protected from the north wind and advantageously exposed to meager measures of sunshine. On several occasions, I have knelt near-worshipfully in front of this modest cluster of brightness. Drinking in deep draughts of flower power from this lone nourishing hope under gray skies.

Meadows have greened to velvet, a startling sight against the stark background. This landscape is a study in contrasts, verdant carpet ringed by snowcapped mountains and skeletal sentinels of maple and birch.

I should be more grateful for meadows' majesty, but I am deeply dispirited by the view from my kitchen windows. They overlook the woods, and the forest floor is still blanketed with dead leaves. Brown, brown, awaiting true spring's renewal.

As April surrendered to May, a few sunny days dawned bright. But winds blew raw with winter's edge, and the sun was winter-weak. It has been too long. I am greedy. Sun-bright is nice, but not enough. I want warmth.

A new edge of desperation came in with May—the sure knowledge that warmth and blackflies will arrive at the same time. Canceling each other out and driving me back indoors.

It's just not fair.

Walking through the woods, it appears that this endless wait for spring has been as hard on the trees as it has on me. Whole trees have fallen . . . as if they could hold out no longer and fell in defeat. Our usual pathways are blocked by their massive corpses. It is not some illness peculiar to our forest. Down the highway and on back roads, we see more toppled trees than in previous years.

My imagination's fancy sees these downed trees as nature's winter-weary soldiers surrendering in exhaustion, having lost all hope that balmy breezes would e'er blow again.

This personalization of the trees' demise is somehow comforting. If even the trees have fallen to the rigors of this lingering winter, my own malaise feels less absurd.

And so I watch the slow progress of barely budding trees with steely intent. "Leaf out, leaf out," I growl in part prayer, part curse.

For comfort, I stand in awe before a small cluster of miniature daffodils, and get down on my knees to gently touch their soft, golden petals.

daydreams of spring

I am not a frilly, frou-frou woman. But when the sun shines and I am basking in a warm spot on the back porch, I long for cotton dresses.

This whim breezed through today, with the realization that I am deadly weary of bundling up against the cold. It's darn difficult to feel feminine through a North Country winter.

I've tried, heaven knows. I've scoured shops for winter wear in bright, light colors. I have even scored a few. My penultimate triumph was a winter coat in a yummy raspberry shade. It brightens glowering days.

Cheery colors help. But as long as I'm layered in bulk, encased in pants and clomping around in boots, femininity eludes me.

Back when I was teaching, I could indulge in lighter wear. Functional outer layers could be shed after the frigid, messy trek from car to class. But now that I work at home, I don't have the cocoon of a classroom to go to.

Here in my venerable, drafty Vermont farmhouse, practicality reigns. Trudging down to the basement wood furnace, popping out to the woodshed, keeping the front porch shoveled clean—these routines do not lend themselves to frivolous dress.

The enduring tomboy in me really doesn't mind the rigors of rural living. There's a deep satisfaction in carting armloads of wood from shed to basement. Without doubt, I carry less each trip than in years past and move more slowly, but I chalk that up to good sense.

Stepping outside into the snappy, post-storm air and shoveling snow can be strangely exhilarating. Holding one's own against the elements is a North Country thrill difficult to translate to citizens beyond these borders. But around this time of the year, my feminine spirit awakens with the siren song of spring. I dream of long, light dresses brushing bare legs. I yearn to tote nothing heavier than a handbag.

It doesn't matter that, in reality, donning a dress will not be my initial spring celebration. Nope, I'll be mucking about in the garden. Or pruning the raspberry patch. Or dodging blackflies to find the first green growth in the woods. Still, if I wanted to stroll down the street in feminine finery, I could.

As the seasons cycle, North Country life demands that we move from one set of chores to the next. High fashion isn't high on our lists . . .

Perhaps my frou-frou turn of mind can be blamed on the Academy Awards show. All those women, hair coiffed, draped in elegant jewels and gowns, trailing clouds of silk down the red carpet, prodded some womanly instinct deep in North Country hibernation.

Wouldn't it be fun, just for one night? Maybe we need a Spring Fling here in the hinterlands. A fluffy, frivolous evening . . . a grown-up prom, perhaps.

Something fun, before spring chores demand their due.

on the fritz

It is May 15 and it is snowing. I'd say something obscene, but my editor would delete it.

Anyway, this is the North Country and I'm not supposed to be surprised by any bizarre weather nature throws our way. I wouldn't want the old-timers to laugh at me.

But it's May 15, and it's snowing.

A few days ago, I spoke with someone from down country—where it's almost summer—and she jokingly asked if it was snowing here. "Bite your tongue," I replied.

I hold her personally responsible for today's snow.

I bet if I drove down the hill into Wells River, it wouldn't be snowing there. Doesn't matter. Up here in Ryegate Corner, the frozen north of the North, I will have to scrape my windshield before I go anywhere.

I know this stuff won't amount to much. The snow shovel can, most probably, stay in the barn. Doesn't matter. There's white drifting down, frosting the lilac buds. It's May 15, it's snowing—it's the principle of the thing.

All told, the universe has put my life on the fritz. I am dangerous. I burn whatever I cook. This morning, I walked on the cat. The other day, I couldn't even open a door and go through it properly. I opened and moved simultaneously, smashing my toes, jamming my wrist, and jerking my head back in shock and alarm.

Now I need to visit the chiropractor, my toe cries "hairline fracture," and my wrist aches where it sits on the keyboard.

Yesterday my computer turned on me. It hiccuped strangely and burped rudely through some essential functions. I spent several frustrating hours on automated help lines—"Please listen carefully to the options: They have recently changed to make it even more impossible to comprehend this process or to get any kind of meaningful help whatsoever."

Here's the only part that made sense, delivered in dulcet tones of hearty humanoid cheer: "Our best guess is that you've picked up a nasty virus. Our live customer service representative will help you on a fee-paid basis of a zillion dollars an hour, or you can visit our website."

I visited their website and was transported to the land of TechnoSpeak where English isn't even a second language. I lack the congenital geek gene, so the instructions served only to alarm me further—"your computer will curl up and die if you don't get rid of this bug."

Thoroughly panicked, I called Paige Computer Systems in Woodsville. Dale said Ely could doctor my computer if I got down there straightaway. Luckily, it wasn't snowing yesterday, so I could fly down the hill.

Ely did his technical thing. No virus. But since I had to pay for the office visit anyway, he gave my 'puter a general checkup, did some geeky magic, and sent me home with a happy laptop. Total cost: twenty-five dollars. Blessings be bestowed on local businesses.

I hope your week is going better than mine and that, wherever you are, it isn't snowing.

leafing out

Golly gee, there are leaves on the trees!

I know this sounds simpleminded. I know that my friends who live Elsewhere will question the state of my mental health, but I shall staunchly defend my delight to all comers.

This is a thrill reserved for denizens of the North Country and similar climes. It isn't that we cold-climate country folk are easily entertained. We're just more attuned to natural wonders. Deprivation does that.

We've had nearly seven months of naked-tree gazing. In our context, the reappearance of leaves constitutes a minor miracle.

I drove down to Hanover last week, in what might be regarded as a reverse-direction foliage drive. From atop our hill, directly in the path of Ryegate Corner's north wind, to the heart of the Dartmouth College campus, I savored the progression of leaf development.

Happily transfixed by the passage from fragile, translucent baby birch leaves to the unfolding fronds of maples, I meandered down Route 5, crossed over to New Hampshire at Thetford, and continued down Route 10. It's a good thing I was out at midmorning when traffic was light. I drove slowly, mimicking flatlander leaf-peepers whose fall rubbernecking drives us crazy.

As if the leaves are as happy as I am in their debut, they come forth shouting in colors that are nearly unnatural. The first leaves of spring are a shining yellow-green neon that glows against the backdrop of dark pines.

Day by day, the distant hillsides gradually fill in, like a child coloring inside the lines with deliberate concentration. I have a friend who insists she likes the starkness of winter—when leafless woods reveal views later curtained by foliage. And it is true. With leaves, the landscape changes.

Roads seem to shrink, narrowed by overarching branches ribboned with green. The woods move in more closely around our homes, shielding forest secrets from sight.

Winter clearings become verdant glades. Rivers and streams, once exposed swaths glistening in the sun, are reduced to glimpses you only catch through wind-parted screens of green.

Backwoods homes retreat once again, no longer visible through the trees. I'll soon forget they are there, and will be surprised again next winter when they reappear.

The harsh lines of winter's countryside have given way to leaf-softened shapes. The monotones of frigid months and mud season are relieved by spring's emerging hues. Even on gray days, the scattered yellow of dandelions punctuates green meadows, rainbow tulips' upturned bells ring cheery notes, and wild violets dance purple through the grass.

In days past, black-and-white photographs were tinted by hand. A blush on the cheek here, a reddened lip there. Our North Country shifts into spring the same way—feature by feature, shade by shade, the countryside comes alive again.

So allow me, please, my simpleminded pleasures. It has been a long winter. I have earned my glee.

where has all the music gone?

Once upon a time not so long ago, music was not just a spectator sport. Some of my most treasured memories of North Country life feature a few friends, a guitar or two, and good times with tunes.

I remember a porch overlooking the lush summer countryside. Bucky with his guitar, Vinnie and me with our harmonicas, a jug of hard cider, chairs tipped back, song rising on a gentle wind. From the trees, woodpecker percussion accented the beat. I still feel the warmth—the sun on my face, the camaraderie of creation.

I remember a cold winter's night. A group gathered around the woodstove, the smoky tang of maple logs crackling. Outside, the wind howled. Inside, the dog chimed in on occasional chords. Riffs of laughter accompanied fingers dancing on frets.

No one would mistake the music we made for professional fare. So what? The magic was in the making. None of us had dreams of stardom. We were teachers and truck drivers, construction workers and waiters. We just loved to make music.

I can't remember the last time I shared that delight. A friend and I were talking about this the other day, and it left me wondering . . . Where has all the music gone?

"Everybody's plugged in and passive," Gino grumbled. "*Watching* music on television, *listening* through headphones." Plugged in and passive. Consumers, not creators.

Child of the '60s, I grew up in the era of garage bands and folk guitar. Everyone, it seemed, either wanted to learn or already played. And in my Girl Scout days, the star at the campfire was the one with the guitar, leading us in song as sparks rose into the dark night.

Even if you knew only four chords, you never hesitated to take your guitar to the party. You'd play your four and learn a few more.

Have we become too busy for the magic of making music? Have we taught our children that music is only for a select few headed for superstardom?

Taxpayers slash music programs from school budgets as non-essential fluff—even though research shows that making music literally enhances brain development. Scientists have all sorts of neurological explanations for that, cells and synapses and brain chemistry.

I look at it more simply. Brain cells dance to the sheer joy of music. Happy brains are healthy brains.

The weaving of notes is an alchemy beyond our ken. Food for the mind, solace for our souls. A mini-vacation. A prescription for what ails you.

Bucky and Vinnie have long since moved away. Somewhere out there, nestled in the North Country hills, I bet there are other people who hanker to play for pleasure. If you're reading this, contact me. Please.

Have harmonica, will travel.

spring fling

Oh, spring! Dressed in new vibrant, lush foliage, some trees bring to mind grand ladies in opulent ball gowns on their way to an elegant party.

And no town around throws a spring fling quite like Newbury.

From the northern point of the old Placey (now Huntington) Farm, south to the old Page (now Johnson) Farm, flowering crab apple trees line the road. Given the right conditions, these unassuming trees turn Newbury into a pink fairyland of delicate enchantment.

There has never been a Flowering Crab Festival, and there never will be. So brief is this glory that one must be poised to appreciate it. One rain shower, one strong wind can destroy the ethereal magic before it reaches full splendor.

Last year, I drove through Newbury just after the party was over. I cursed myself for the busy-ness that had driven from my mind the approaching time of beauty. I promised myself it wouldn't happen again. I vowed to stay attuned to the signs, to remember that an exquisite experience awaited.

On Mother's Day, Neil and I drove slowly into Newbury, ooh-ing and aah-ing at the preview on the outskirts of town. Then we parked at the school and walked through fairyland, giddy with the sights and scents.

I wouldn't trade that walk for a byline in *The New York Times*.

This flowered exuberance is a bit of small-town sorcery—ordinary people creating an extraordinary vision. In the spring of 1969, the Jolly Workers 4-H Club of Newbury, under the direction of Marjorie Deming and beautification project leaders Mr. and Mrs. Leland Wooding, set out 270 flowering crabs.

The 4-H kids sold the trees to individuals and town organizations and helped plant for people who couldn't manage by themselves. Not all the trees survived, but the legacy is undeniably magnificent. A few of those kids are grown and still live in Newbury; eleven families of those dozen Jolly Workers are still represented in town.

How proud they must be, along with everyone who bought a tree. What deep pleasure they must feel to have had a hand in creating this heritage of nature's resplendence.

They certainly have my profound gratitude. The quixotic jubilee is no less glorious for its fleeting nature. Indeed, the flowering crabs of Newbury remind me to make space for beauty in my life . . . and that is a magic all its own.

Many thanks to Pat Rhoads and Ginny Swenson for helping me get the history straight.

mother's aprons

Dreams are strange things. Like messages in a bottle tossed into the seas of our somnolent minds, they sometimes bob to the surface in great detail. I woke one morning, thinking of my mother's aprons.

In my dream, I was giving a dinner party. I wanted a nice apron to wear for the evening and thought one of Mom's would be perfect. But as I mentally ran through all the places the aprons might be—tucked in the cedar chest, folded among the sheets—I realized I hadn't seen them for a very long time.

Then I realized I no longer had them.

I felt a piercing sense of loss so acute its sharpness wakened me. The distress accompanied me into consciousness.

I am a keeper of things, a collector of memories. My grandfather's gold retirement watch rests in my mother's cedar chest, alongside his Shriner's ring. When Dad died, I kept several of his shirts—I wear them with bittersweet affection when I garden. Mother's fancy evening purses accompany me on special occasions.

I never roll dough, yet her rolling pin has a prized place in my kitchen. Her wedding crystal serves wine to my guests. But I do not know what happened to those aprons. Did I give them away as some useless artifact of a lifestyle long gone, I wondered in the dream's aftermath.

My mother was a woman of a generation that *wore*

aprons . . . and now, families struggle to even sit down to dinner. And when they do, how often is it a dinner cooked from scratch, with all the mess that entails? Microwaved food isn't very messy. Macaroni from a box cooks up cleanly.

Recently, I saw an item on the news about a town that decided the rush of life had become too much. Collectively, they decided to cancel all after-school activities and evening social events once a month. On that evening, the town would sit down to dinner together. Parents and children, families together.

This town wanted to reclaim the "family dinner" tradition that was an unquestioned daily routine of my upbringing. When I saw this, I first thought, "How wonderful," then "How sad" that it should take a community movement to wrest from life an hour to break bread together.

I see my mother's aprons in memory. Everyday colorful cotton aprons with indistinct stains even Clorox couldn't quite erase. Fancy aprons she wore for dinner parties, barely functional, with deep ruffled netting like a bridal veil.

I dreamed of Mother's aprons, icons of another time. A hungry dream for slower days, rich with gravy.

A dream in memoriam for a generation of women whose homemaking arts were misunderstood, devalued in the storm of "liberation" that followed . . . whose daughters now have a new appreciation for the complex grace of a family meal.

the vermont way

Our yard has been ugly. The artesian well installed late last fall left us with the granddaddy of bald spots stretching across the north end of the house, near the perennial gardens where we usually sit in nice weather.

Then, as winter's snow piles threatened spring floods in the basement, we hired Jeremy to move the mounds away from the foundation. As good as he is with his big rig, it left deep gashes, as if an angry clawed monster had used the front lawn for a scratching post.

When the grass started coming up, the yard looked pathetic. Unsightly ruts ran every which way, and spring flowers bloomed next to naked ground.

Do we need a layer of clean fill? Who would haul and spread it? How much would that cost?

I added such items to my domestic to-do list, where they languished amid urgent or ordinary day-to-day tasks. Mostly, I just looked the other way when I walked from the car to the house, feeling that our yard was a blight on the countryside. A measure of our failure as country folk.

We eventually made it to a local garden store, thinking we'd at least buy some grass seed. There we learned that grass is complicated stuff.

There was a dizzying array of seed to choose from. Apparently, we were supposed to "match" what we already had.

What kind did we have? If we planted a different kind, would the lawn look strange?

Then there were fertilizers. Some grass seed had it mixed in, but other products claimed that was insufficient for verdant growth . . . And there were spreading gadgets, for seed, for fertilizer . . .

Neil and I left the store, baffled and feeling stupid, overwhelmed by the science of grass.

About that time, a Vermont farmer friend came over and I confessed our yard care anxiety. I was ready for anything: dry humor at our incompetence or a detailed laundry list of utterly intimidating procedures.

Well, said she, you could go to all that trouble with fill and recontouring the ground. Or you could just wait and see how much grass comes back. Then you could toss a few handfuls of grass seed in the worst places. If not this year, then next year, she figured, it'd all probably take care of itself.

"That's the Vermont way," she said.

I was relieved—I had been given dispensation. It was okay for things to look awful. It was okay to let nature take its time.

Things look better now. The claw scars healed themselves. The ruts have mostly leveled out. Neil just finished raking and tossing some seed (by hand) around the shrinking wasteland.

Maybe this will do the trick. Maybe it won't.

We'll just wait and see.

there's a tornado
in georgia, but will it
rain in vermont?

When Neil and I bought our house on the hill in Ryegate Corner eight years ago, we moved from cable country to television Never-Neverland. Two stations, folks. Count 'em. Two.

We could probably get more with an outside antenna, but high winds are common up our way and the maintenance shock of owning our first home was bad enough without worrying about that, too. Besides, a few spectacular thunderstorms convinced us we didn't want an antenna competing with the lightning rods.

So we learned to live with Channel 8 out of Maine and Vermont ETV. The TV upstairs occasionally pulls in Channel 3 out of Burlington, but only if the wind is blowing just right, if you jiggle the rabbit ears to perfection, and if skies are clear. We found TV-alternative ways to entertain ourselves and have adapted pretty gracefully to the limitations, except for weather reports.

The Maine station acknowledges New Hampshire weather, but Vermont gets only an a-yuh sort of mention. Over time, we've learned that if the Maine-predicted weather front is moving north, we're likely to be in the midst of whatever they're anticipating. If the front is moving south, it generally takes a day and a half to get here. East–west patterns are too ornery to figure out.

On ETV, they don't do weather, except documentaries on hurricanes and historically significant snowstorms.

This year we decided to buy one of those small satellite dishes and looked forward to expanded entertainment and improved weather reports courtesy of modern technology.

What we got was 175 stations, give or take a few . . . and no local weather.

I don't understand the Weather Channel. What they call "local weather" covers someplace in the Midwest, and just about every time I tune in, I catch "Pacific Weather Update." It's nice to see what my California friends are experiencing, but I live here. When the actual weather people do the national weather, they seem to think the East Coast stops somewhere around New York. Vermont doesn't even rate little symbols to give me a hint of what's to come.

I've been startled by dire weather warnings flashing across the bottom of my television screen, preceded by an attention-getting tone resembling an electronic alarm clock, guaranteed to jump-start a resting heartbeat. I catch my breath, poised for action in the face of impending natural disaster . . . until the affected areas are listed. The threatening tornado is headed for Atlanta (CBS out of Georgia) or the heavy storm is a distant southern fury (NBC from Carolina), and I feel like a damn fool.

ABC comes out of New York, but heaven knows their weather patterns are not our own, or even as distantly related as fourth cousins once removed. We can tell you the three-day forecast for Neil's folks in New Jersey, but don't know if we should close our windows before going to work.

It's an odd thing, being members of the global community. We can watch the nightly news from Japan, but I'm left wondering whether to water my garden or if this dry spell will break. I'm trying to build the radio habit and look for weather in local papers, but I miss the visuals.

On TV, I can be anywhere but here.

Welcome to the Twilight Zone of modern technology.

seasonal rituals

As if nature could read the calendar, the first day of summer brought hotter temperatures. Though the days had previously been warm, nights were so cool I still had flannel sheets on the beds.

Summer arrives later in Ryegate than it does less than ten minutes down the hill in Wells River or Woodsville. Perhaps you've long since switched to cotton sheets, broken out the fans or put in air conditioners.

Such tasks can be perceived as irritating chores, or they can be seen as rituals of the season—the rhythms of our lives. I find quiet comfort in the cyclic tasks of seasonal shifts.

I go out to the barn where the fans are stored. A bird has built a nest on a beam. As I enter the barn, the bird and I startle each other. It alights on the painted wooden figure of a sorcerer. The sorcerer's pointed, glitter-glimmering hat is now crowned with our feathered tenant. Very Harry Potter. My laughter alarms the bird into fluttering retreat out the barn door.

The nest is an architectural wonder. Stuck on the face of a beam, the wad of fuzzy mud gives no hint of an opening. This bird is not a neat builder—bits of nest have been falling for days. Neil has moved the tractor from beneath it so the mess lands on the floor instead of fouling the machine.

As I carry a standing fan back through sunny heat to the

house, I notice that, despite the rain we've had, the grass is dry and crunchy.

Since we store the fans in the barn, I don't clean them before I put them away. Maybe that's a rationalization. We cover them with plastic, but it just feels right to start summer with freshly cleaned fans. With two dogs and a cat, animal hair gets pulled into the safety grids and collects dirt. Being allergic to dust, the last thing I want is to fire up a fan and blow dust all over the house.

I enjoy small mechanical tasks. Disassembling the fans, I am pleasantly meditative. Hands busy, mind empty. It is satisfying to see the white plastic blades emerge pristine from their layer of grime.

Madness and mayhem may be afoot in the world, but my fans are clean.

Tomorrow, I'll open the cedar chest I inherited from my mother and take out the cotton sheets. I remember, with a smile, how she gave me the chest when I first moved away from home. She hated that chest, a "proper" girl's present when she turned fourteen.

She had wanted a new shotgun.

Chores, yes . . . but they sing the songs of our lives.

garden scrapbook

One of my earliest memories is of my mother on her knees in the gardens of my childhood Virginia home.

It was the '50s, she was a Southern lady, so she wore pink flowered gardening gloves and a housedress with an apron as she trimmed the rosebushes. Her long, dark hair pulled back in a bun and crowned with a braid, she'd hum and dig in the decorative borders of our backyard.

Even I knew these moments were snatched from brownie baking, women's service clubs, choir practice, and carting children hither and yon—the full life of full-time moms in the days before "working" motherhood.

She never grew vegetables, but we had crab apple trees. By some sorcery, she transformed their bitter fruit into delicate jelly in steaming, pungent pots. And so it was that even in a post–World War II suburban neighborhood, I grew up with an awareness of the land's bounty in roses, irises, and jams.

I planted my first pansies in Pennsylvania when I was in third grade. Pansies, because I needed their happy faces. My family was miserable in our new, unwelcoming town.

In my floral ignorance, I hoped they would draw humming-birds as in my grandmother's West Virginia garden where hollyhocks grew taller than me. There, jeweled birds darted diamond-bright in the summer sunshine among the yellow tomatoes my grandmother taught me to love.

My grandparents' home was a row house with a narrow corridor backyard in coal country. There, my grandfather bestowed gentryhood on his family because he was not a miner. He sold insurance in a land where the whistling, lumbering passage of coal-filled trains sang my summer lullabies.

I have my own gardens now, carved out of Vermont tropical-lush forests clamoring up the hillside to reclaim every small bit of land I've tamed. The wild has its way. Columbine and lupine mingle with carefully cultivated perennials, native sisters moved in at the land's will, not mine.

Flourishing flowers have been a wonder to me. The first year, I watched winter kill and despaired. But in the spring, the garden proliferated. After another season of bounty, I thinned the growth and expanded the flower beds without having to purchase a single plant.

In jeans and sneakers I fight the ferns that would engulf my flowers, humming in Skin So Soft–scented shirts culled from my father's closet after he died. Blackflies and myrtle don't give much ground. The only roses I have are gifts from a gardener long since gone, who perhaps like myself was surprised by their appearance—pink, wild, and lower to the ground than their stately, well-bred sisters.

I have no hollyhocks here, but bee balm grows tall and calls hummingbirds. They grace our garden like small, sleek angels. Their presence creates a connection with the gardens of my childhood . . . humming memories of the women before me who also kneeled on dirty knees and smiled.

strange skies

Life gives us magic moments. In the North Country, these moments often involve nature.

The visiting falcon perching on the porch roof. Two pairs of black dragonflies dancing in tandem down by the brook. The rosy glaze of alpenglow on distant mountains.

Living here has taught me to drop everything and grab these quixotic gifts. The falcon takes sudden flight. Darting dragonflies vanish in the next breath. Alpenglow is a transient trick of light easily erased by a passing cloud.

"Come see!" is our urgent code for fleeting natural phenomena. No time to explain what or why—whatever it *is* could be whatever it *was* in a heartbeat.

I'm fascinated that this immediacy exists in counterpoint to the underlying slow rhythm of North Country life. The seasons turn, and turn again. If you haven't managed to pack away your winter clothes by now, it isn't worth the effort. Soon, the late-summer evening chill will have us reaching for those sweaters. Let it go.

But when a snowy owl perched in the tree smack-dab in front of my kitchen window, I was there instantaneously.

Some things simply cannot (and will not) wait.

Take rainbows and the shifting light of sunrise and sunset. The full arc of a double rainbow fades faster than the time it takes to put away that last dish. A whimsical lavender sunset cloud turns common pink while you hang up a shirt.

And so it was that we recently surprised Rod and Gail who were driving by our house at sunset . . . They spotted Neil and me romping atop the rock wall bordering our front yard.

The sky, you see, was bizarre. Abruptly abandoning the movie we were watching, we dashed outside and clamored up on the flat-topped wall for a better view.

We beheld an eerie sky. Just above the western tree line was a bright strip of gleaming, greenish gold. Above that was a bank of huge clouds illuminated by the strange light. The clouds had jagged edges, needle-sharp and glittering. In contrast, the northern sky was utterly dark with foreboding thunderclouds.

The wind blew weird, expanding greenish gold clouds right at us. If the hairs on the back of my neck didn't stand on end, they certainly wanted to.

Suddenly the line of trees to the west was brought into sharp focus in the uncanny light—as if seen through finely adjusted binoculars—and the leaves of one maple glowed phosphorescent.

Then radiating beams fanned out like spotlights, pointing to the highest heavens, and the peculiar greenish tint was gone. The trees returned to their normal appearance.

"Oh, wow," was our immediate, if inarticulate, response.

A year from now (well, heck, maybe next week), I won't remember what movie we were watching. But those moments on top of the wall, watching the peculiar sky, will forever be an Oscar-equivalent memory.

an embarrassment
of berries

When we bought our place, we inherited a raspberry patch. It's probably as old as the house. I suspect more than a century of berries has come out of this unruly thicket of nature's glory. Even old-timers can't name one of the cultivated varieties here.

This plant produces berries the shape and size of a thimble. Nearly an inch long, perfectly conical and sweet, they are almost seedless. Really. This is not just a proud momma bragging. I have witnesses.

Picked warm in the afternoon sun, the berries melt in your mouth like raspberry cotton candy newly spun . . . so delicious it nearly breaks your heart.

Like much else in the North Country, the patch has a mind of its own. Disdaining orderly ranks, it marches to the beat of an untamed drum. The cane grows like small tree branches—tough and sturdy, rising nearly six feet if unpruned, bending and weaving together in leafy embrace.

Untended for many years, the patch was a tangled nightmare of dead cane and new growth. "Mow it down," many advised. "There's nothing else you can do."

But I love raspberries. As snarled as the poor patch was, its twisted jumble offered a veritable embarrassment of berries. Red riches glowing in golden sunlight. To sacrifice such bounty seemed a sacrilege.

I knew nothing of raspberries. I had never tended a crop nor cultivated any plot of land. So, for the first three seasons, I simply observed.

Gradually, the patch revealed its secrets. Cane that looks dead in the early spring is dormant and will bear summer's berries. It is easiest to distinguish dead cane in late spring by the absence of leafy shoots. Emerging growth is inconveniently underfoot but cannot be cut. Those plants will bear next year's berries.

In those first years, I picked by wriggling through the thicket on my belly like a combat soldier moving under barbed wire. Flipping onto my back on the damp ground, reaching up through twisted branches to grasp one berry at a time.

Finally, I began cautiously to care for the plants. I was terrified I'd violate one of nature's raspberry rules and ruin the gift given to me.

But the patch tolerated my down-country fumbling and flourished. My crops now come in gallons, not pints.

Every summer, day after day, my kitchen counters are covered with cookie sheets and platters of red gold. Filled with wonder, camera in hand like a tourist on my own land, I take pictures of the harvest.

I can no longer imagine a winter without raspberries. The rattiest raspberry in August is a miracle in March.

There is magic in the land.

firefly romance

During a recent late-night drive back from Burlington, on the stretch of road outside Barre, I saw tiny streaks of yellow light in the tree line.

I had just returned from the wilds of Manhattan, where lights twinkle near and in the distance. I was momentarily bewildered. I knew there was no little city back in the trees.

Then my country self kicked in, and I remembered. Fireflies. Against the dark foliage, their luminescence threaded ribbons of yellow as the car sped by.

Fireflies, faeries of the summer woods.

Firefly magic always makes me smile. Certainly the Creator and Mother Nature collaborated with Humor, fabricating a glowing creature whose urge to mate advertises itself with such illuminated glee.

Anyone who grew up in lightning bug territory has childhood memories rich with golden-green glow. How long could you bear to keep their blinking bodies imprisoned before you set them free to dance their light in the dark again?

Where were you when you caught them in jars with hole-punched lids? Who were you with?

Forgotten friends flicker back to mind in firefly reflections. Summer's temporary playmates, united by vacation, as fleeting yet entrancing as the fireflies themselves.

Grandmother's back porch. It was probably a small garden,

but it was large to me then—towering hollyhocks and profusions of plants both edible and decorative. I first went face-to-face with a hummingbird there, frozen in place by his intent inspection before he determined I was not sweet enough and darted off.

But the soft nights are what I most remember. Three generations gathered by firefly light. The comforting creak of wood-on-wood as rockers rocked and the grown-ups watched us dance after lightning bugs with determined delight. We could not understand why they did not join our dance.

As I watched the golden tracks from the car, I pondered. What power these little bugs have to retrieve the past from memory's shadow, illuminating each detail, glowing with warmth. For a moment or two in firefly spotlight, they all live again: Grandmother Ru, Granddaddy Russell, Mom, Dad, and my companions of childhood's lost time. Their laughter echoes in my ears, dear faces are wreathed in smiles and soft summer winds blow sweet.

For a moment or two in firefly light, I dance again in the dark.

harvesting patience

I'm in training for raspberry season. The rigors of preparation are as daunting as any faced by an athlete getting ready for the big game.

Go ahead and laugh. But last year's bumper crop nearly did me in. It's foolish to expect to shift from a sedentary routine hunched over the computer to hard labor picking berries, and I was a fool.

You can only get away with that when the blush of youth still gilds your rose. My roses stopped blushing years ago—but the mind is slow to catch on. I blithely expect to go from relative inactivity to daily, unremitting physical exertion with nary a muscle twinge.

Last summer's harvest disabused me of that illusion. If not for the grace of berry-picking friends, gallons of red treasures would have rotted on the canes, while I mourned in achy, enforced rest. I swore this year would be different.

I know better than to think I would dedicate myself to an exercise regimen. I've always hated exercise. In my athletic days, "exercise" was something you did briefly to warm up for the *real* fun—the sport itself.

A sit-up is a sit-up. It isn't an activity. I walk to get from one place to another, or to pass some contemplative time in the woods. I watch people "power walking" with purposeful determination and am filled with admiration. But exercise as its own reward is a concept my psyche refuses to embrace.

What better way to get in shape for raspberries than by working in the patch. So for the past several weeks, I've been in raspberry training. Not only cleaning out the dead cane— an annual chore—but also attacking the invading witchgrass, putting in new metal posts, stringing more supports, creating new rows. Cutting, digging, pulling, straining, reaching.

The first day of this endeavor, I was able to keep at it for only an hour. This aging body's early warning system then notified me of potential significant damage if I did not cease and desist. At once.

I listened. Strategic retreat is the action of a wise warrior.

Feeling like a wimp, I waited several days before going back to work. My inner coach gave me the go-ahead when I could reach for a dish on an upper shelf without wincing.

My next session lasted two hours, with a shorter recovery time. The session after that, I marked four hours, with a rest period between two-hour stints . . . and it just keeps getting better.

The patch is looking pretty good. The raspberries are ripening, and so am I. Go slowly, I keep reminding myself. Getting older doesn't mean I can't do the things I want to do. I just need to do them differently.

As a memorable tee shirt advises, aging is not for wimps . . . and only the young can indulge in impatience.

On I go, row by row.

summer bright and dark

The day dawns clear, with piercingly blue skies and a fiercely blazing sun. On waking, I close all the windows to capture the cool night air. The promise of a hot, humid afternoon is heralded with birdsong.

In the harsh sunlight, the trees and grass shout with verdant vitality. The flowers in my garden radiate with intensity. Yellow blooms are small suns fallen to earth. Wild roses sing deep pink unfolding. Daylilies smile orange starlight.

A perfect day for laundry, I think. Energized and ambitious, I imagine clothes strung on the line, saving electric dollars.

By the time I've hung two loads, the sky is darkening. A wind has blown up, tossing the leaves to reveal their silvery undersides. The threatening storm is oppressive, like a deep sadness lurking in the heart that cannot be relieved.

It feels as if there is no air, as if it has been sucked into the descending darkness, into the gathering force of the storm. Flowers take on an eerie glow in the gloom, faint spots of color, like multi-hued candle flames fading before guttering out.

The clothes whip in the wind, headless bodies twisting and turning, arms flailing, empty legs kicking. Stephen King would love it.

The darkness deepens. Day turns to night. I switch on the kitchen lights.

When the rains come, they come with a vengeance, surging with punishing force. Thunder growls, then crashes as I rescue the clothes. I give them safe haven on the shower rod, where they rest quietly after their tortuous dance.

Lightning flashes and cracks with savage abandon. Strobe lights in the heavens. An unseen force wielding a bullwhip of celestial proportions. I am glad for our lightning rods and wonder if some of the explosions I hear are trees being hit in the woods.

It is a Shakespearean storm. Picture King Lear on the moors, mad with disillusioned grief, shaking his fist at the heavens.

The metal roof resonates with rain rhythms. I am no longer ambitious. Time to curl up with a good book. The dogs lie by my side, the cat crawls into my lap. The pack has gathered. Against the wildness outside, there is safety in numbers.

Three chapters later, I raise my head to see sunlight streaming through the windows.

The storm has passed.

My creature companions follow me downstairs, outside onto the back porch. Glittering diamond-bright raindrops wink from leaves in a forest of waterborne jewels. In the air is the freshness that comes with a world washed clean.

Down by the brook, black dragonflies come out to play. Darting through shimmering grasses, meeting and circling, separating and meeting again—a square dance on the wing.

I pull up a chair, and sit in the shaft of sunshine beaming through the trees.

bath and beyond

There are shower people, and there are tub people—or so I've heard tell.

I'm both. Showers are for getting clean. Baths are for luxuriating.

When you're house hunting, real estate agents tell you to beware of falling in love with any single feature of a home. Makes sense, I know—but the antique, claw-footed tub in the upstairs bathroom featured prominently in my enthusiasm for our house.

Me and that tub. It was love at first sight.

Long, wide, and deep, that old bathtub sang its siren song. It's a good thing I liked it; it probably weighs an immovable ton. None of this contemporary fiberglass nonsense. This is a serious porcelain-over-steel job. In the winter, it takes a good deal of hot water to warm that baby up, but once filled it holds the heat for a long while.

I call it my therapy pool. I figure it has saved me thousands of dollars in therapist's fees. Bad day? Fill 'er up, add a few drops of rose oil, light some candles, set a glass of wine on the tub-side table, play some gentle classical music, and an hour later it's a whole new world.

I'm an expert bath connoisseur. I can read in the tub without getting books wet, and I have a method for plugging up drain holes to give myself an extra inch and a half of water without sloshing over the sides.

There isn't anything much you can tell me about the art of bathing.

Or so I thought. Then a new friend came to visit. She oohed and aahed over my tub—they have an efficient, modern house, featuring only a shower. Out in the garden, she admired my wild roses. We love roses. We have neither knowledge nor patience for cultivating them, but wild roses come back every year with no care at all.

They're smaller than their hothouse sisters but just as sweet. As we bent to drink in their scent, she noticed the piles of petals in the grass, fallen pink gems against the green.

"Those are great to put in your bath," she commented.

I was stunned. Roses and tub for some twelve years, and never the twain had met—despite my preference for rose-scented water. Isn't it odd that we keep garden and bathroom so categorically separate?

Petals on water. A delightfully incongruous sight, pink fairies come to play. Raise an arm, and they beach themselves on skin—soft, light kisses that swirl away on small tides of gentle waters. Skim cupped hands along the surface and gather handfuls, breathe deep the essence of roses, still sparkling with sunlight.

Child's play is filled with wonder. Everything is new. Petals on water, and I'm a child again. Weaving an enchantment of simplicity, the union of bath and beyond, ordinary things creating something fresh.

The roses have gone by now. But as I walk my garden, I consider other possibilities . . .

holly's hollyhocks

Once upon a time, there was a rock wall. Hollyhocks grew along the wall, tall spires swaying in the wind.

I remember climbing the wall, securing toeholds between protruding rocks. It was a daring climb then. We'd sit on the top, my friends and I. There we would make hollyhock dancers.

Pluck one blossom. Insert a toothpick through the center. The flower becomes a skirt, and we'd twirl our dancers in the summer sunshine. Sometimes holding a dancer in each hand, we'd create whole ballrooms of flaring skirts, telling stories of ladies in pink and purple skimming across the floor.

There was a man who owned the wall. He lived in the house not far from where we sat, spinning our dancers, our stories, our dreams. He was a nice man, but he scared us because his hands shook and he always looked sad. My mother told me his hands shook because he had a disease called Parkinson's. There was no reason to be afraid.

She told me he was sad because, years back, his whole family had died. His wife and children were in a car that stalled on railroad tracks. A train came.

He was lonely, my mother said. He liked children. She would take us into his big house to visit. He always had something sweet to drink and cookies for us that he would lay carefully on the table with those trembling hands. I remember the picture on the mantel. A soft-smiling woman sitting between a boy and girl about my age, each one tucked in the protective curve of her arms.

That scared me, too. That they had died.

Sometimes when we were on his wall dancing our dancers, we would look up to see him standing at a window. He would raise his hand in a shaky wave. We knew if we waved back he would invite us in for cookies.

But we were afraid. Even cookies could not entice us into his sad and silent home. We visited him only when Mother took us by the hand.

Several years ago, Neil and I had a rock wall built along the edge of our yard. From the day it was finished, I was haunted by a desire to see hollyhocks rising against its stony face. But more pressing projects took precedence, and seasons passed.

Two years later, I visited my friend Holly's house, where hollyhocks grew tall and strong in pinks and one purple so deep it was nearly black. Memories rushed in. I asked. She gave.

They wouldn't bloom the first year, Holly said, and she couldn't promise I'd get a purple one. Hollyhocks change colors, she told me.

I watched them last summer, broad leaves barely above the ground. This summer, they blossomed. There is a purple, almost black. I think of the grieving man with the shaking hands. There are pink ones, too. I think of the joy his wall gave us.

I smile when each new bud opens. I smile at the green stalks swaying in the wind against the stony wall. It is a memorial. My apology for childhood fear . . .

My thanks for hollyhock dancers.

almost a farmer

I'm back in the bushes again.

The raspberries ripen languidly in this awkward summer. Too little sun, too little rain, too much rain all at once.

I'm back in farmer mode. Checking my crop daily. Watching the skies. Snatching berries from the threatening jaws of mold and insects. Soothing aching muscles as best I can.

It is good, this annual shift to crop and land. All else becomes secondary. The fruit of the earth will not be put on hold. Cannot be scheduled into agendas.

I am out in the patch. Now I live closest to the land. The computer is silent, email unanswered, ringing phones ignored.

I do not "play" at farming. The red treasures are too great a gift to take lightly. My winter stamina depends on these frozen riches, reminding me that brighter seasons will come 'round again.

It may sound absurd that from my plot of raspberries I feel connected to those who farmed before and to those who farm still. But there it is. I will not apologize for this, nor for my awe of folks who carry the burden of farming full-time . . . who *always* watch the skies, their labors in Nature's capricious hands.

In the patch, the elements become elemental . . . and I ponder the North Country's heritage.

Settlers came here to till the soil. They cleared land without chain saws, much of it now reclaimed by forest. They heaved stones from new fields by hand. Through wicked winters and short growing seasons, they carved out a life in the wilderness, amid isolation we can only imagine.

They say that most Americans don't have to count back more than three generations to find farmers in the family. (It might be four or more now, so far have we come from the land.) As I gather the harvest, I feel a link with my paternal great-grandparents who farmed fields in Russia and Poland. Carrying berries into the kitchen for freezing and boiling, I feel connected to my maternal great-grandparents who farmed first in Scotland and then in America.

This is good. To remember that roughened hands, not corporations, once fed families. Remembering what a miracle food is—wrested from the grip of Nature, which cares not if bellies are full or empty. Cares not if the labor breaks backs or spirits.

So each berry is a triumph. Wrought by earthy forces beyond technology, a tangible trophy of the sweat of the brow, patient determination, and Nature's rare grace. Each berry spinning a thread between past and present, touching the spirit of those who brought their own food to the table.

Everything I eat, the milk I drink, takes on a special quality now. I wonder by whose hands food comes to my table and what it cost them to feed me. How many nights did they pray for rain, beg for sun, hope for the best?

I am happy to be back in the bushes again.

Talking with a dairy farmer friend one wet summer, I bemoaned my disrupted harvesting schedule and my untended raspberry patch. She listened impassively . . .and it dawned on me how much greater a burden the sodden weather placed on her.

What with all the rain, she hadn't been able to get out into

the fields. The rhythm of chores was on hold, corn unculti-
vated while they waited for the land to dry. North Country
farmers have a short season as is, and the loss of a few days
poses problems, never mind losing a couple of weeks. They'll
be playing catch-up till winter, when the weather drives
them inside.

Considering the challenges she faces in the fields, I felt
pretty idiotic and downright small for worrying about my
raspberry crop. But then she smiled.

"Well," she said with the calm characteristic of her kind,
"you'll just have to be behind like the rest of us farmers."

I was so flattered to be numbered among the stewards of
the land that I forgot my frustrations, shrugged off my com-
plaints, straightened my shoulders, and stood taller.

"A-yuh," I said. "I guess I will."

Nature moves to the beat of her own drum. We who would
take something from her can only dance to her rhythms.

raspberries revisited

This strange summer has played havoc with my raspberry routine. The fruit began to ripen a good two weeks ahead of schedule—long before I was prepared for the labor-intensive days of harvest.

Nature cares nothing for the scheduled plans of puny humans. She offers her abundance as she will.

And ripe berries wait for no man . . . or woman. Ready or not, here they come.

Harvesting this year has been a race between the mold, the insects, and me. Given the heat, humidity, and rain, no sooner would a berry ripen . . .

And they're-rr-rrre off!

Comin' down the stretch, it's Furry Mold in the lead. Scurrying Ant is close behind, running nose-to-nose with Persistent Wasp, but coming up hard on the outside rail is Harried Woman . . .

When one rare temperate day finally dawned, I had an unbreakable appointment that kept me from the patch until late afternoon. I dashed home, stripped, basted myself with Avon Skin-So-Soft, donned appropriate berry-picking attire, secured my hair out of tempting reach of creepy-crawlies, slapped on the patch-hat, grabbed the cut-down plastic gallon jug-buckets, and headed out.

Several hundred berries later, as dusk darkened the thicket,

I refused to give ground. An entire section remained unpicked. Given this summer's past performance, who knew when another such day would come?

As the shadows deepened, it became impossible to tell which berries had reached the perfect deep red state of ripeness. Frustrated, I considered grabbing a flashlight. But that seemed too absurd for even the most fanatic berry lover.

In a final gesture of surrender, I stuck my hand blindly into the foliage . . . and felt three perfect berries plop softly into my palm. Ripe fruit will do that. Fall into your hand if you gently cup a cluster just so.

I had to smile.

It isn't always necessary to see the fruit. Sometimes, just reaching into the darkness is enough. But your hand has to be open.

perfect peaches
and other mysteries

When life gets too complicated, my mind takes refuge in contemplating the minor mysteries of life.

Why do people turn away from the price of steak, but spend two bucks on a handful of potato chips without hesitation?

Why do my dogs want to lick my clothes only when I'm dressed in my best?

Is there a plastic wrap gene? Some people handle the stuff with ease, while others can't touch it without creating a tangled mess.

What is the secret of a perfectly ripened peach?

I love peaches, but they are a cantankerous fruit. Unripened, the peach is hard. Eating it is not unlike chewing a bar of soap. Properly aged, a peach provides an exquisitely flavored, melt-in-your-mouth delight.

Choosing the potentially perfect peach is an art. My mother had the gift. In some arcane manner, she would select the most promising peaches, bring them home, and nurture them to their peak.

I haven't had a properly ripened peach since Mom passed on.

My peaches tend to rot before they're ripe. I've tried the ripen-in-a-brown-bag-with-a-banana trick. I have set them in the sun, in shade, in warm spots and in cool. I've talked to them nicely and serenaded them with classical music.

At best, I have managed a half-ripe, half-hard peach. Nibbling the juicy delight with surgical precision to avoid nicking into the bitter portion.

On very special occasions, my mother would prepare an elegant Southern treat. She'd fill her wedding crystal champagne glasses with a good California dry champagne and float several perfect peach slices in each glass. Then we waited with anticipation while the peach marinated and flavored the cold bubbly.

I have my mother's wedding crystal now. And champagne is easy to come by. But those perfect peaches remain a mystery.

One of the nice things about getting older is acquiring a knack for acceptance. I accept unknowables with more grace than I could have even imagined two decades ago.

When people claim they want to hear the truth but cannot themselves muster the courage to tell it, I can smile instead of frothing at the mouth in frustration.

When the guy on the bar stool next to me bitterly complains about a fraction-of-a-penny increase in school taxes but moments later laughs about dropping forty bucks at the bar on Friday night, I can shake my head in wonder instead of screaming.

When what can go wrong invariably does, at the most inopportune time, I mutter "Murphy's Law" with only minimal truculence.

But the mystery of peaches haunts me with irritating persistence. Every time I toss out another unripened, fuzzy-with-mold failure, I feel a temper tantrum coming on.

And please, don't even get me started on cantaloupes . . .

perfect peaches — reprise

This is a small-town tale.

Nearly two years ago, I wrote a column titled "Perfect Peaches and Other Mysteries." In it, I recounted my woes with this most delicious fruit—particularly my inability to master the art of ripening peaches before they rot.

I recalled with mouthwatering detail the exquisite peaches my mother had provided, noting that I hadn't eaten a perfect peach since she passed away.

Several weeks ago, I stopped by Pierson's farm stand in Bradford to buy strawberries. As I shopped, I chatted with the folks there. The woman laying out produce asked, "You're Nessa Flax, aren't you? You write that column for the paper?"

I admitted I was, and did.

"Remember that column you wrote about peaches?"

I really had to think about that—there had been a lot of columns since then. Finally, I nodded.

"I meant to call you back then but didn't know how to reach you . . . We get beautiful peaches from Pennsylvania. You won't have any problem getting them to ripen perfectly. We'll be getting them in soon," she said.

Amazed and flattered that my column would stick in her mind for so long, I hastened to assure her that I would *love* to know when they came in.

"You can always reach me through the *JO*," I said. "If you

call and leave a message with Connie, she'll email me and I'll make sure to get right down here."

I happily trundled my strawberries to the car, thinking I should let Connie know about the impending peach alert. But I was busy with summer and it slipped my mind.

Sure enough, a week or so later an email arrived from Connie. "Sara Pierson called to say the peaches are in," she wrote, clearly baffled as to the newsworthiness of this bulletin. "She said you'd understand."

I fired off a reply, filling in the blanks and thanking Connie for acting as messenger. The timing was perfect. I was headed down off our hill in Ryegate Corner for an appointment that very day. I could stop at Pierson's on my way home.

There they were. Crates of peaches. Peaches unlike any I had encountered in grocery stores. Peach-colored peaches. Peaches emanating a blissful aroma. Peaches that were not rock-hard, but were ever-so-slightly soft to the touch.

Sara Pierson was right.

I had no trouble ripening these peaches. I even succeeded in picking out some that were already ripe and others that would ripen over the next several days.

Peaches so juicy they had to be peeled over a bowl. Peaches that melted in my mouth. Peaches that made my taste buds stand up and do a little song and dance of glee.

Perfect peaches.

And a perfect small-town tale.

reveling in ryegate

Once again, the Civil War comes to town.

The afternoon before Ryegate Heritage Day, white tents of a time long past sprout in green meadows behind the Meeting House. From my windows, I watch them rise, stark against the clear blue sky.

It is impossible to continue my ordinary chores. I walk down the road to witness the transition from today into yesterday.

It is a strange and wonderful sight. Uniformed soldiers mill about with newly arrived blue-jeaned travelers. Artifacts are unloaded from pickup trucks as the living tableau of another era takes shape.

I meet Amanda Page of the Springfield Art and Historical Society. Already garbed in the long, hoopless work dress of the Comtu Falls U.S. Sanitary Commission, she sets up camp. With her is Emily Stringham, a self-possessed teenage intern who has been in the program since eighth grade. In a puddle of ground-sweeping skirts, Emily coaxes wood splinters into flame with the fan of a proper young lady.

From Amanda, I learn that the commission was a forerunner of the Red Cross, tending to Confederate and Union soldiers with equal dedication. From Emily, I learn that living history beats the heck out of hanging out at the mall.

Below the rise, men string pickets along the tree line behind the Grange. We talk horses. Since I know little, I ask a lot.

Is that horse with spots on his rump an Appaloosa? No, his owner tells me with a straight face, it's just a white horse.

I feel foolish.

He later explains, with a grin, that since there were no Appaloosas in the Civil War, "I just call 'im a white horse."

That night from my living room, I watch the campfires burning. Soft laughter floats on the cool evening air. I feel cozy with my new neighbors. The next day, I awake to cannon fire. They have brought their world to mine.

Saturday night, Neil and I walk in the twilight down to the dance. Elegant ball gowns, swaying hoops, and handsome dress uniforms transform the Meeting House into an intersection of now and then. Scattered among proud soldiers and their ladies in the grand march are my neighbors in blue jeans and Bermuda shorts.

We learn to waltz. With much laughter, visitors living the past teach locals stuck in the present the steps of the Virginia Reel. Scenes from *Gone with the Wind* unfold—whirling skirts and gentlemen bowing—only better, because I am here.

Oh, the high spirits! Stomping to music, participants turn wooden floorboards into a communal drum. Costumed and uncostumed revelers share a raucous celebration of dancing joy. Rebel yells mingle with Yankee shouts. Everyone sings, *"Oh! Susanna, don't you cry for me . . ."*

Rare and wonderful hours slip by in merriment—a gift from reenactors who bring such passion for what they do. A gift from Barbara Watts of South Ryegate who works so hard to make it happen. A gift from volunteers who feed armies of participants. A gift from every sponsor who contributed.

I thank them all.

wanting mother

What I find most irritating about death is that it is so stubbornly permanent.

Few things in life are absolute. Mostly, life is an ebb and flow in shades of gray. You can be a little late, days can be a little hectic, but you can't be a little bit pregnant or a little bit dead.

For some inexplicable reason, I miss Mom a lot lately. She died five years ago, and I find myself increasingly nettled by the fact that she is still dead.

I keep wanting to ask her questions. Like how she made her biscuits so fluffy, or if she was scared when she first moved to New York from a small West Virginia town. I want to know, in intimate detail, her feelings the first time she laid eyes on Dad, and whether she sometimes felt like her house had tentacles that wound themselves around her, threatening to suck the very breath from her body.

I long to ask if she doubted her sanity when the hormonal craziness of midlife struck, and how she got that tart tang in her pound cake.

Did she truly enjoy dyeing Easter eggs and decorating Christmas cookies all those years, or was she graciously providing fodder for our fond memories?

I wonder if she was angry at having to carry so much of the domestic burden during those years when Dad's job kept him on the road. Or did her era bestow upon her some grace of acceptance beyond my generation's capacity to fathom?

I want to ask her how she coped with the burden of love. Did she break into a cold sweat when Dad was late, picturing him plastered on the pavement? Was she ever calm as she watched her children walk out into a world filled with danger?

I keep wanting to tell her things, too. Like how I now understand why, as she got older, she refused to watch shows about distressing realities of life. Murder, genocide, domestic abuse—she turned them off.

"But Mom," I protested with the fervor of youth, "these things happen!"

"Indeed they do," she replied, "but they are not the foundation for entertainment."

I judged her an emotional escapist. I know better now.

Mostly, though, it's the questions that haunt me. Did she still feel like a girl inside though her mirror presented an aging image?

How did she feel in the tumultuous '60s when the values she held dear were challenged and ridiculed? Did she ever forgive the early women's movement for making motherhood seem trivial, second-class?

Decades after her own parents' deaths, I remember Mom saying she never stopped being lonesome for them, so I know she missed her mother, too.

Did she have questions tinged with regret? And what would they have been? I have no answers.

Even if we take care and ask what we can while we can, the truth is that some questions do not arise until we reach later stages of our lives, years after someone has passed on.

There is no remedy for this.

I guess that's why they call them the blues.

when the bough breaks

A few years after we moved here, we had a grand old maple tree taken down. We hated to, but it loomed over our house. A logger friend told us he suspected the tree had been dying for years and was dangerously top-heavy, so down she came.

Our friend was right. The trunk was hollow from the ground up, through three-quarters of its height . . . Saved by a savvy woodsman.

At the same time, we asked him to look at another majestic maple a little farther from the house.

"Yup," said he, "she's dying, too."

We were new to land- and homeownership then. With the unseasoned perfectionism typical of rookies, we asked if we should have it removed as well. He regarded us stoically, then spoke in the tones one would use to educate very young children.

"No, when she falls, she won't hurt nothin'." Pointing, he said, "When she falls, she'll land in the brook, right about there."

He tilted his head, regarding the tree. "A bad storm might take 'er, or she could live on for ten years, maybe more. No call to take 'er down before her time."

In the decade or so since he made that pronouncement, storms stripped the tree of branches. The ailing trunk splintered and broke and began to rot. Finally, all that remained was one glorious branch, parallel to the brook and our back porch, a horizontal line across the kitchen windows above the sink.

Flocks of mourning doves, twenty or more, lined up along that branch for several years—until the falcon came. Nuthatches mined the bark, and for a while two varieties of woodpeckers lunched there regularly.

No matter how ragged the trunk became, every fall, the leaves on that branch would turn with the same joyous gaiety of younger trees.

One clear and windless Saturday a few weeks back, I bustled into the kitchen, intent on a series of room-to-room chores. What I caught out of the corner of my eye stopped me cold. In utter silence, nearly in slow motion, that branch was falling. The span of kitchen windows was like a movie screen on which the familiar horizontal line simply slipped out of sight.

In those split seconds, I was baffled and oddly frightened. It was as if the sky itself was falling. Then came a mighty splintering sound—wood tearing away from wood—and a thundering thump as the branch hit the ground.

I rushed to the back porch, to see Neil standing not twenty feet from where the branch had landed. He had taken the dogs out to walk their usual path along the brook.

"Did you *see* that?" I cried out stupidly, before it dawned on me precisely where he was standing.

"Wasn't it *something*!" he called back.

Then it registered. Where he stood. The branch lay in one of the dogs' favorite wading pools.

"Yeah," I whispered, "that was something . . ."

after the bough breaks

For the fourteen years we have lived here, a majestic maple tree has graced our home. Rising from the steep bank leading down to the brook, she shaded the back of our house. Her leafy veil protected us from the heat of the afternoon sun.

Even after age and decay had reduced her to one reaching branch, the rooms in her shadow were a naturally air-conditioned refuge at the height of summer. We'd put fans in front of those windows, drawing the tree-cooled air into the house.

She's gone now. And from the moment she fell, our world changed.

A span of sky has been unveiled. Stark in its emptiness, expansive in its reach. From the sitting room where I spend quiet time with good books and journal writing, my view is newly crowned with blue by day and stars by night. Across the brook and into the woods beyond, I see aspects of trees I've never seen.

Standing at my kitchen sink, I observe the altered flight paths of birds approaching the feeder that dangles from the back porch beam. Nuthatches who used to take their seeds up to that outstretched branch now fly to trees farther away. Mourning doves, who preened on that sunny perch, now fly in from some way station out of sight.

The air is filled with wings.

In the late afternoon, light streaming into the bathroom

radiates so brightly, spilling into the next room, that I keep going in to turn off lights I must've left on. It will take time to curb this impulse.

It is hotter now on the back porch, throughout the after-noon and into evening. The laundry I hang on the lines dries faster, and sections that used to be shaded late in the day are now prime territory. But our cool evening retreat to the porch chairs must wait until well after sunset.

I think of winter. The snow usually piled up on the porch steps leading to the garden, dumped in avalanches from the intersection of house and porch roofs. I wonder if the unveiled sunshine will change winter's snowy landscape. I wonder if I will be warmer at the kitchen sink, where the old uninsulated wall offers weak protection from frigid winds.

The sun sets as never before. I am startled by large squares of sunlight stretching across the kitchen floor. Crystal prisms on windowsills above the sink send rainbows dancing in new patterns on walls and ceiling . . .

I am bemused by the awareness that, in her absence, the majestic maple is more present than ever.

With each transformation, every new shaft of light, I remem-ber her with affection.

lessons from the garden

Once upon a time, a friend of mine had a poster hanging in his office.

"Sometimes I sits and thinks," the ungrammatical prose read, "and sometimes I just sits."

More than three decades later, I remember the smile that surprised my face when I first read those lines. It struck me as particularly amusing since my friend was a professor at an Ivy League college.

I remember feeling oddly reassured . . . as if I had been given permission to *not think*. In the ensuing years, I've discovered that not thinking is an art. Just try it. It is not easy.

Not doing isn't easy, either. Especially this summer. North Country summers are fleeting under the best of circumstances. This season has been merely a flicker in our wistful imaginations.

What makes our summers so short is more than the number of days. There's so much to do in the fair-weather months; weeks fly by on the wings of one set of chores after another.

And thus it came to pass that I was tending to long-overdue weeding one rare lovely day. As I attacked the encroaching offenders, lists of other tasks revolved through my mind . . . and I sat down to catch my breath.

It was late afternoon. The sun glittered gold through the leaves, danced off the stream below in silver reflections. Puffy clouds lazed across a sky-blue canvas. Deep magenta bee balm waved in the breeze.

I felt myself slow down, sinking more heavily into the chair. I noticed how startling the pink phlox looked against the background of deep green leaves.

Stillness settled over me.

I realized I couldn't remember the last time I had simply sat in my garden. Just sat. Not noting what needed to be done. Not planning what flowers to plant next.

And so, I sat.

Flashing iridescent green, a hummingbird came to the bee balm. Its thrumming vibrated through my stillness. I watched the darting, hovering creature as it fed, watched as it was joined by its mate. To my utter shock, I heard for the first time hummingbirds chirping.

I watched as one came to rest on the branches of the small tree behind the flowers. Hummingbirds don't sit for long, but years in my garden have taught me that to see one stop *at all* is a rare gift. I breathed softly.

The first hummingbird took flight and its partner alighted on the same branch while the other fed. Then they traded places again. I watched this dance for several moments, utterly delighted. If I had not sat quietly, the performance would not have happened.

Native Americans believe that hummingbird's medicine is joy. They believe hummingbird feathers can open the heart. Without an open heart, they say, you cannot taste the nectar, the pure bliss of life.

Those hummingbirds surely brought me joy, reminding me that, to taste bliss, sometimes we have to just sit.

thunder and lightning

The rumble comes from far away, indistinct. It could be the echo of a large truck, a high-flying military jet, or our big dog Devin resettling himself upstairs.

"Was that thunder?" we wonder.

The night silence settles into an eerie stillness—that strange calm before the storm. Then the wind comes. Trees first sway in waltz time and move rapidly to a rumba, leaves rustling like swirling taffeta skirts.

The thunder rolls in. No mistaking it now. Imagine a celestial wooden floor with mammoth boulders moving toward us and away in waves. We hear and feel forces gathering.

Finally, the first flash of lightning. As if, from somewhere beyond the sky, a flashbulb of mythic proportions fired. In milliseconds of illumination, the countryside is cast in blue-white light.

This is the theater call. We turn off the television, grab some treats, and settle into our front-row seats on the enclosed porch. The large, long windows are open—we are almost outside, but safe. When the rain comes, we are misted with wind-blown spray.

High on our hill in Ryegate, we have open views over the meadow to the mountains—a vast expanse of sky on which the lightning plays. Nothing matches an evening's storm entertainment.

Every show is different. Like birders who record each sighting, we collect variations of lightning witnessed during more than a decade here.

We have seen truly frightening balls of lightning. Forks flashing pink, thick clouds backlit with flares of electric white. We've seen bolts shoot toward earth, heard the splintering crack of a tree being struck, then crashing as it falls in nearby woods.

Twice, our lightning rods have captured a bolt and given us the bizarre experience of feeling the walls shiver as the energy ran to ground.

Even if there's nothing new, the show's still grand. But tonight, there are new thrills.

Sheet lightning in rosy hues. We ooh and aah in reverent whispers. At center stage, horizontal lightning, snaking and branching in a race across the sky. But strangest of all on this evening are the lightning bugs.

Between the cracks and flashes high above, lightning bugs flicker in the meadow. They flit about, undaunted by the rain. As if they are conversing in code with their light-cousins in the heavens.

We don't remember ever seeing this back-and-forth of tiny lights with the broad and blinding strokes above. It is a sweet sight—a dance of the minuscule and the majestic.

My imagination dances with the bugs and the bolts.

Do the bugs envision the lightning as a grand rival for their ladies' attentions? Have they become so flickeringly active in a valiant effort to prove their worth against the big boys up there?

What a lovely evening's entertainment.

the raspberries ripen

For nearly fifteen years, I've been entranced by nature's sorcery in my patch. I've been told that raspberry plants last about seven years, then they're done. Not mine. They keep coming back and starting new mini-forests beyond the confines of the main plot.

Faithful readers have received many a summer's tale of my adventures in what I've called "the grandmother of all patches." It is not a civilized place. I do not have neat rows to walk and pick. It could, more accurately, be called a raspberry forest.

My forest is still not civilized, but it's worlds better than it once was.

Hard labor is involved in maintaining the patch. Dead cane must be removed in the spring. Pruning keeps the plants at a height I can pick without standing on my tiptoes. Stakes and string must be tended to keep paths open. Encroaching witchgrass must be pulled.

Yet each year when the fruit ripens, I feel that the bounty of ruby gems far exceeds the time and energy I've invested. It's still magic. I watch the flowers become small, hard white kernels . . . then watch them grow larger. They first turn orange-red, then finally transform into deep red, juicy fruit.

Hundreds, thousands of them—every one a miracle. I move through the patch in wonder. Berries high and berries low.

Shining in the sun, hiding under leaves. At peak harvest, it takes four hours to pick the whole patch if I am alone, another two to put up the day's treasure for winter.

In recent years, I have become less inclined to do this day after day, week after week.

Thank heavens for Phyllis, who is as much of a raspberry fanatic as I am—and picks faster than I ever will, though she has nearly twenty years on me. She keeps what she picks. In exchange, Phyllis gives me jars of her incomparable jam. She makes special seedless batches for me. I ration the glorious jars carefully, through winter and the dreary mud season that holds spring hostage.

If your jam-eating life has been restricted to store-bought varieties, you cannot imagine the intense delight of Phyllis' ruby spread. Sight, smell, touch, taste: The senses celebrate.

And between her farm chores, Holly picks whenever she can. She rewards me with heavenly raspberry pies, delivered in deep winter months. Her piecrust is a marvel. Flavorful, thin and crisp, never soggy as fruit pies often are. I don't know how she does it. I am happy to simply savor the delectable mystery.

Grab your buckets, ladies. It's that time again.

(*. . . And time for me to take a break from the column while the harvest is bountiful. See you after all the picking's done.*)

starry, starry night

In the midst of the boil and bubble of North Country life, there are moments that stop the heart with awe . . . and we know with utter contentment why we live here.

We know why we suffer a spring as brief as an eyeblink, an insect population bent on inflicting torture; why we slog through the sanity-challenging despair of mud season, the icy complications of winter; why we endure the frenetic pressures of summer.

We understand why we accept the "you can't get there from here" bedevilment of rural life and the complexities of nothing-to-do but too-much-to-do with too-far-to-drive-to-do-it.

One night before the full moon, I experienced such a reminder of bliss.

It was late. I couldn't sleep. The air had cooled, so I went to close a window. As I reached up to lower it, I saw the stars. A zillion pinpoints of light against a perfectly black sky. I ducked under the curtains to expand my heavenly line of sight, but it was not enough.

Beguiled, I was drawn outside. On the way, I flicked the porch switch. No artificial light should disturb the scene.

The Milky Way arches over our driveway. I stood beneath it, entranced by the sparkling diamonds spilled in concentrated profusion against the velvet dark. As I marveled, the mournful lowing of cows from Bill and Jenny's farm echoed across the meadows.

Though I could see no moon, a cold, blue-white moonlit quality illuminated the landscape. The distant tree line was cast in silhouette, spiky treetops etching a ragged edge against the sky.

As I walked up the driveway, away from fans rattling in the windows, the chorus of crickets intensified as if someone had turned up the volume. The Big Dipper dangled hugely above Ted Clark's house as if to empty its contents over his roof.

Mesmerized by the still, dark-bright of the night, I wandered up the road. No bugs bothered me. The air was sweet, spiced with a green-growing fragrance released by nightfall's alchemy. I passed through shadows cast by starlight, more subtle than sun-shadows, but as distinct.

I looked back toward our house, comfortable on its rise, guarded by sentinels of birch, pine, and maple. Circling slowly, I surveyed the scene from humped mountains sensuously rolling in the east to the tree-lined ridge in the west. And above it all, that impossible, improbable, better-than-Disney, star-studded sky.

This spectacle is ours. We live nestled in what has, elsewhere, been cut down, plowed under, paved over . . . places where lights wash away the stars and quell the song of night.

We live nestled in nature's embrace. It's just outside our doors.

clear view

I hate to say this out loud (or in print), but summer wanes.
There it is.

Have you tossed another blanket on the bed? Closed windows against the cold night air? Seen the first tree blush orange?

The season begins its waltz into fall. It is a gentle time. As I write this, I'm basking in the second of two classically beautiful North Country days. The sun and air are crystalline, a perfect breeze tosses the leaves, the midday temperature is summery.

With winter looming on the other side of fall, such days feel magical, oddly ephemeral and glorious all at once. I sense a vague wistfulness as summer slips away, a touch of nostalgia for June and July.

I've had a good summer and am loath to let it go.

Perhaps we never lose the childhood joy we felt when school was over and September was unimaginably far away. I have not forgotten the sense of foreboding as the specter of school opening laid its cold hands on my unstructured days. This is the only explanation I find for my inner shift from playful ease to *getting down to business* . . . as if my mother had just told me we were going school shopping.

Oh, those dreaded words.

How strange. These many decades later, I can still feel my

stomach sink with that pronouncement. Can remember how a lightness left me. Recall the feeling that something had been taken from me, a spell shattered.

No matter how warm the sun, the last days of August simply did not have the enchantment of June. I remember wanting, trying to recapture summer's sorcery, to no avail.

And so it is today.

But, older now, I sway more softly in this seasonal waltz. Gently, I begin to let summer go. I let the season be. There is no potion to transform August into June, no fairy dust to sprinkle on my psyche. In this acceptance, I can hear August's symphony, appreciate her song.

Nor am I, as in years past, leaping into that edgy "before the snow flies" mentality. I caress these crystalline days.

I wash windows.

I am clearing the way for every bright moment to shine through. I want a sparkling view of the sun illuminating green trees and meadows. When raindrops dance diamonds in the last of day's light, I want no dirt to dull the sight.

If I could put my arms around the crisp light and blue skies of these days, I would.

I cannot, so I wash windows.

transitions

changes

Writing "Rambling Reflections" has often put me in strange and sometimes awkward situations.

Because of the personal nature of my writing, when I meet someone new who reads the column, they greet me as if I am a longtime acquaintance. I don't take offense. They do, in fact, know a great deal about me. About my thoughts, about my life.

What makes it awkward is that I know nothing at all about *them*. While I'm touched that my writing makes them feel close to me, it's like meeting a stranger who has read my diary.

Here in the North Country, where people are a bit reserved, my column has served as a nice icebreaker. At the bank, grocery store, or local eatery, someone will hear my name and launch into a conversation about columns they've especially enjoyed.

This is rewarding for a writer. It has also given me opportunities to engage with folks I wouldn't otherwise have met.

Then there are my friends who read the column but are quite busy. We don't have the chance to get together often, yet they feel in touch with me because of the column. My friend Jenny put it best when she once said, "I keep forgetting it's a one-way 'conversation.'"

But none of these situations is as strange and awkward as

my present one—feeling the necessity to "announce" in print significant changes in my personal life.

Because my home with Neil—the brook, gardens, woods, and raspberry patch—has played such a prominent role in my writing, I see no way around announcing our breakup and the sale of our house.

As with most long-term relationships that come to an end, the outward final stages are anti-climactic. Our separations during the past several years have been known only to intimate friends. But when the FOR SALE sign goes up on the lawn, what has been private becomes public.

I'm very fortunate to have found a new place in Ryegate Corner, just up the road from the house I've lived in for seventeen years. It is important to me to stay here—Ryegate, quite simply, is home. Who can say what makes a place and a community feel like "home"? Whatever that is, it's what I feel here.

The past several weeks have been a wild whirl. Shifting from intense emotional chaos, I have plunged into the realm of real estate. Realtors, buying, selling, lawyers, bankers, forms, and files.

I found a new house where the land sings to me, a place that makes it possible to leave this house and land I have so loved.

We all need an anchor when changes rock our world. My centering force has been the meadows, the woods, the hills and mountains . . . and the people who make this corner of the North Country *home.*

recipe for metaphor

We had a monumental storm last week. Teddy-dog and I were visiting a friend in South Ryegate. We sat on the porch and watched the celestial light show for hours.

Well, my friend and I watched. Teddy mostly slept. He's remarkably unimpressed, undisturbed by the most cacophonous storms.

The thunder rolled and crashed, the rains came, the electricity went on and off, but eventually it was quiet. The nearly full moon radiated softly from behind heavy clouds as I headed back to Ryegate Corner by the back road up over the hill.

I drove cautiously. Dirt roads can be treacherous after heavy rains.

I was driving more conservatively than is my custom. This was fortunate. I came around a curve, and lying fully across the road was a dead tree, felled by the storm.

Now, here is where it gets silly.

I stopped the car (startling Teddy) and stared helplessly at the roadblock. I was completely flummoxed. I looked at Teddy, Teddy looked at me. My thoughts ran like this . . .

Oh, my, what am I going to do? There aren't any houses around. No help nearby.

It's dark. I don't have a flashlight. I should keep a flashlight in the car.

I'm wearing a long dress and sandals. I should keep a pair of hiking boots in the car. I'll have to turn around and go back to Route 302. But I'm closer to home than to 302.

Then, from some deep wisdom place within me, a small voice said, "Get out of the car and move the tree." I might add that this small voice spoke in tones that implied, ". . . you fool."

There, in my car, in the dark of night, on a lonely back road, I laughed out loud. At myself. Teddy looked at me questioningly.

I got out of the car, held up my skirt above my ankles, and with mincing steps tried to walk without squishing my sandal-clad feet in the softer muddy places. The wet road dirt rubbed against my toes. The tree was long, but not hugely thick. It had clearly been dead for some time, so I figured I had a shot.

I reasoned that I didn't really have to *carry* the tree—I just had to lift it enough to pivot it around to the side of the road. Which is what I did, skirt hiked up around my waist as I bent and grabbed the thicker, trunk end.

It took less than a few minutes. Yes, it was heavy and awkward. But, really, it was do-able.

I stared with abashed satisfaction at the tree lying on the roadside. Simple.

If you think I'm now going to turn this incident into a metaphor for how we respond to obstacles along the back roads of our lives . . . well, I sure could. The thought occurred to me.

But I'll leave that up to you.

saying good-bye

This house I have lived in for the past 17 years is 164 years old.

As I prepare to leave, I feel humbled to have been a part of its history. I know this sounds hokey, but there it is.

The house was built in 1840, the same year Britain's Queen Victoria married Prince Albert. While hand-hewn beams were being set in place on this farmland in Ryegate Corner, Sir Charles Barry began building the Houses of Parliament in London.

According to 1841 statistics, seventeen million people then lived in America. These days, that's approximately how many folks live in Florida.

I toss out these facts in an attempt to frame the sweep of history laid in the foundation stones, the years that whisper through the walls. More than a century and a half is a difficult concept to grasp.

I have been influenced by living here. Rereading past columns, I witness my wonder at the wisdom of old-timers who knew how to best situate a house to maximize the natural assets of the land. Early generations that lived here left evidence of earthy knowledge worthy of respect.

Until a few years ago, our water came from a dug well out in the woods, on the other side of the brook. Soon after we moved in, we had a local mason rebuild the crumbling brick above ground. When he saw the stone-lined well, he commented that it had been decades since he'd seen a well as old as ours still functioning.

Those pipes from the woods, under the brook, and up the hill into the house never froze, never broke. During many dry spells when others' wells failed, ours kept going. During two of the worst seasons, the granddaddy of dowsers—Paul Sevigny of Danville—diverted water veins to refresh the well. And it kept going.

I can't know exactly how old that well was. But it served us admirably, courtesy of an ancestor on this land who was rich in earth wisdom.

There are so many memories here that spoke to me of a time and workmanship from an era past. In 1992, when a drunk driver miscalculated the curve and plowed into the house at an estimated fifty-five miles per hour, his pickup truck was stopped by granite foundation sills and a tree-sized corner beam.

I'll never forget Ryegate Fire Chief Gene Perkins' comment: "Way-ull, if this'd been one of them new houses, truck woulda' gone straight through and come out t'other side."

Indeed.

What will it be like to live in a fourteen-year-old manufactured house after living in this venerable grande dame of a place?

I do not know. But this I do know—the lessons and sensibilities the old house awakened in me have become a part of my nature.

I take them with me.

stuff

Imagine this. You're moving from your present residence into a place approximately one-third the size.

What furniture will you take, what will you sacrifice?

Your new place is not simply smaller in square footage. Subtract two-thirds of your current closet and shelf space. Now open every drawer. Kitchen, bathroom, wherever. Most of that stuff has to find a new home. Not your new home. Somebody else's.

This process entails a merciless life review. All those little projects you were going to get around to, the hobbies begun and abandoned . . . at every turn you face the detritus of your intentions.

You encounter the remains of every collectible phase you've been through. In the kitchen, you track numerous attempts to improve your diet through special pans and gadgets.

Gifts you didn't really like (but you were too tactful or cowardly to say so) gather dust or sit in prominent places of obligation. Then there are the ribbons, bows, and gift bags your thrifty nature inspired you to save.

Our life histories are reflected in our stuff. Our psyches are revealed in dark closet corners.

Here's the good part. Forced to downsize, you can make new choices about everything you own—assuming you have the requisite fortitude and ruthless courage. These qualities are more easily acquired when you're the one who will pack and unpack every odd thingie and whatsit you keep.

You can ask yourself, "Does this item belong in my life *now*?" In answering that question, you discover self-revealing things about who you've been, how you've lived, how you *want* to live, and who you want to be.

The short version of what I've learned is that I just want less stuff.

Another redeeming feature of this grueling process is the joy and liberation that come with giving stuff away. Selling things is nice, but giving things away has a special kick. There are places happy to receive whatever usable items you have. There are people who need what you no longer want.

I take the greatest pleasure in giving away items of good quality. I know that in a thrift shop somewhere, this lovely thing will delight someone. I spent enough years thrift shopping to remember the thrill of finding nice things, not slightly damaged but like new.

Clearing out stuff clears away the past. It creates space for what is unfolding in the present. Parts of my past are dear, and mementos of those times are not a burden. But I've also come to understand that much of what is precious to me is not confined in china, cloth, or any material item.

The memory of my dad's grin is more beloved than his over-sized chair. Remembering the trill of my mother's laugh more magical than her half-dozen antique pitchers.

Letting go, you get more than you could've imagined.

moving and murphy's law

It's quite possible that natural forces of chaos are awakened by change . . . setting them free to run amok.

Weekend before last, my foster son Justin came home. The plan was for him to remove the considerable amount of stuff he'd been storing in the barn. A generous friend, Tom, offered his barn. Afterward, they would help with my moving preparations.

Good plan.

That Friday night, as Justin, Tom, and I lingered over a late dinner, Teddy-dog had a close encounter of the intimate kind with a skunk.

Flashback. When I was new to dog ownership and new to the North Country, I didn't handle my first dog/skunk adventure well. Fawna was squealing piteously, writhing in obvious agony, and I panicked. My immediate impulse was to help my beloved pet—I let her into my apartment.

The outrageous assault on my olfactory senses was overridden by nurturing instinct.

Fawna proceeded to roll around furiously on the living room wall-to-wall carpeting, rubbing her face into the rug in a frenzy. By the time I listened to my nose, it was too late.

This time, I didn't make that mistake.

I knew tomato juice isn't as effective as it's cracked up to be, nor did I have it anyway. I rushed to Earl Proulx's *Yankee*

Home Hints and received the wisdom to wash the animal in equal parts vinegar and water.

The quarter cup of vinegar I had clearly wasn't going to be sufficient. The store is far away. I considered who lived nearby that I might call at 10 p.m. My farmer friends tend to be up later than the average Ryegate resident, so I bothered Jenny. Tom jumped in his car, drove down the road, and received (at arm's length) her available supply.

I wrapped Teddy in a towel and took him into the bathroom, put him in the tub, and proceeded with the wash. By the next day, it was clear that vinegar is only moderately effective. It was also clear that skunk essence is undoubtedly one of the most powerful components on earth.

The bathroom stank. The house stank. Teddy still stank.

Blessings on Erin Nelson and the Ryegate Small Animal Clinic for the following "recipe" every animal owner should keep:

Mix 1 quart hydrogen peroxide with ¼ cup baking soda and 1 teaspoon dishwashing detergent. Erin informed me that this recipe was given to them by state officials for use on skunks sent to them for rabies testing.

It's a winner. If I could douse my house in the recipe, I would.

Tom and Justin moved the stuff from barn to barn, but the weekend mainly featured skunk-cleaning follow-ups that continue to this day.

Now, would you like to hear the story about how my car developed rattling and grinding noises so frightening I had to leave it at Mike's for repair?

The forces of chaos romp on.

With the madness of moving and Murphy's Law, don't look for a column next week.

thank you

As my moving adventure slows from frenetic rush to the measured pace of settling in, I reflect on the blessings of friends.

It was a mad whirl, preparing for two house closings in one day. Getting out of one house and into another in a matter of hours was logistical insanity. But it turned out to be a remarkable experience of controlled chaos wrapped in laughter and good cheer.

Landmark events in life completely disrupt our routines. The death of a loved one, marriage, the unexpected ending of a long-term relationship, moving—there is good reason why these transitions top of the list of stressful events.

Some people understand how challenging such times are and generously interrupt the rhythm of their own lives to help. These folks are shining stars in the firmament of friendship.

"People surprise you" may be a cliché. But, oh, how true it is. I received help and support from folks quite new to my life, and old, close friends turned their lives over to me.

My friend Dee, who lived in Newbury for decades, came down from Maine. She worked nearly 'round the clock for two weeks, first in the old house, then in the new. Tom gave up any semblance of a life of his own and brought along his friend Tim, whom I've only known for a few weeks. They masterminded the final stages of the move and packed a U-Haul with expertise that would make a professional blush.

People underestimate how huge the "smallest" effort is to someone who is overwhelmed by all that needs doing. I received apologies from my elves that they could not do more, but each task they completed significantly lightened my load.

When landmark events unfold, it doesn't take much to mean a lot.

Craig and Ellen from Housewright Construction showed up at critical moments to provide just the needed touch. With perfect timing Cid, the superintendent of the building in Woodsville where I had my studio, appeared with a strong-backed friend.

Walter hauled heavies. Holly held her breath as she wrapped delicate heirloom china. Marie deconstructed framed paintings too large for my new place, preparing them for storage. Phyllis cleaned and scrubbed.

Connie and Cicely at the *JO* set me at ease as I abandoned my column. Robert donated a roll of blank newsprint for my infinite wrapping, delightfully done without the grimy, inky residue of newspapers.

It's impossible to imagine how I could be sitting here now, writing this column in my new little home on the hill, without the generosity of all these people.

Despite the labor and stress, the past several weeks have resonated with the spirit of an ongoing party. And I was the honored guest.

My new home and my new life have been baptized by the blessings of friends.

getting to know you

For seventeen years, I lived in a house by a brook.
Except for a brief time in deep winter when the stream was silenced by ice, the song of water dancing over rocks always played in the background.

At my new house, there is no brook. I am nestled close to the woods, in stillness. In the quiet, I'm experiencing a new symphony of sounds.

One day, as the wind tangoed through the trees, the chattering of late-season leaves led me to believe it was raining outside. It was only when I lifted my head from unpacking and looked out the window that I understood what I was hearing.

Later, when the wind slowed to a waltz, I sat on my deck watching leaves meander to earth from lofty heights. As each leaf joined crisp cousins on the ground, I heard the distinct *click* of their reunion.

Then there was the day I heard a loud rustling from the forest floor. I peered into the woods with great interest. Surely some sizable wild creature must be moving by to make such a racket.

It was a squirrel.

For seventeen years, I lived in a house where sunsets were hidden behind a hill.

At my new house, leaf-stripped trees have unveiled a view of the western sky. Sunset spectaculars will be winter's consolation. Already, I have been driven from chores by glittering gold-edged clouds demanding witness. Brushstroked clouds of lavender and pink drift across a sliver of turquoise sky in the moments after the sun slips out of sight.

Just beyond my house, there's a wonderful road for sunset walks. I bundle up, put Teddy on the leash, and carry a flashlight to alert cars to our presence in the dusk. There is not much traffic here, but people tend to drive fast along this stretch . . . though I cannot imagine why they would want to.

Up the road, as the sun paints a canvas of glory in the western sky, pastures give an open view to the eastern mountains. Teddy sniffs delightful new scents while I turn my head from left to right, not knowing which beauty to behold.

For seventeen years, I looked across the meadow to my neighbors' houses. Their lights radiated companionable comfort at night.

At my new house, there are no neighbors within view. The moon and stars are my companions; silhouettes of pines are sentinels encircling me. When it's overcast, I am embraced in deep dark . . . unless Teddy wanders across the backyard and trips the sensors, flooding the night with light.

Then the yard is a study in light and shadow. Shadows of the hammock and its anchoring pines are sketched across the grass. The edge of the forest is illuminated, its secretive depths beckoning.

Seventeen years is the longest I have ever lived anyplace.

It is so new to be someplace new.

at home
in the woods

summer's sweet slide

The other day, I saw a maple beginning to turn. Its golden leaves blushed red amid calm green brethren, a bold proclamation of what's to come. There's a subtle shift in nature's energy now, impossible to describe. Some people may scoff— but others feel it, too.

If summer had a voice, it would be an exuberant shout. Wildflowers pop up in infinite varieties, tossing rainbow colors and kaleidoscopic shapes into bright sunny days, glowing in the moonlight. A visual "Hallelujah Chorus," they rejoice in fields and meadows.

As summer slips away, pinks, blues, reds, and purples are outnumbered by swaying goldenrod and black-eyed Susans. Rich yellow hues, indeed, but more like grown-up chaperones at a party compared with the confetti gaiety of kids.

This fall chorus hums. Summer sopranos step back, tenors move to the front.

The evening air cools. Now I can rarely sit on the back porch gazing at stars without a sweater. But each time I regret the loss of summer's dark warmth, I think of the true cold ahead and am grateful to be outside, needing only long pants and sleeves for comfort.

Gratitude is the sweetening emotion as summer slips into fall. When the wind sends its cool message on balmy afternoons, I turn my face to the sun, feel its warmth seep into my bones and savor summer's parting gifts.

From my back-porch perch, I look into woods still curtained with leaves. In my mind's eye, the vision of winter's bare branches and white blankets is vivid. I relish today's green abundance.

Summer gives way to fall with a gentle farewell. As she slides, her numbered days make each more sweet.

Nature's tender turning from this season to the next is a kindness. Summer does not abandon us abruptly—how cruel that would be—but dances us lightly between short sleeves and sweaters. There is something in the North Country temperament that enjoys the dance.

After a recent hot spell passed and cool evenings moved in, I was chatting with a stranger about the weather. (We may be strangers, but North Country folks are bound by nature, and we celebrate this bond in casual conversation.)

Sighing happily, she said, "Oh, it feels good to sleep under a blanket again."

I immediately knew what she meant. Tactile images of curling up contentedly under my favorite afghan came to mind. Smiling, I agreed—and felt the North County fellowship spark between the stranger and me.

If you live here, you have to like change. There's pleasure in the shifting season dance, even as the days begin their march to winter. Maybe our common bond is an addiction to the sweetness of farewells.

fall song

The veil of leaves is gradually dropping. Each day, I see farther into the woods surrounding my home.

In new spaces between the pines and leafy trees, I see more open sky. Glimpses of distant mountains surprise me. Gentle contours of the land roll to greet me.

When breezes blow, leaves chatter as they fall, as if whispering secrets to the trees.

In one of my favorite spots in the woods, lush carpets of gem-bright mosses frost the ledges. I cannot resist. One temperate day, I remove shoes and socks and walk across the moss, carefully, not wanting to disturb its delicate hold on stone.

It is a luxurious experience. The cool, soft moss squishes against my skin, surrendering saturated water like a living sponge. The sensation is like no other. I do not feel the ledge beneath. There is no evidence of my steps, no footprints as the moss reshapes itself in my wake.

With winter consciousness, I am hungry for the open air. Between tasks, I slip outside to sit on my back deck, or front porch, at all hours. In light and dark, under clouds and in the sun, standing even in misting rain, I say a long good-bye to temperate times of outdoor comfort.

Sitting quietly one morning, I have my first encounter with the deer.

What primal instinct sends a message that I am not alone? I look up from my book to see a young deer feeding where the woods meet my yard behind the garage. It raises its head and flicks its ears at my slight movement. I hold very still.

We are face-to-face, perhaps two or three car lengths apart. I regard it. It regards me. Apparently, I am no threat because after moments it lowers its head and continues to feed leisurely, nibbling the greenery at the yard's boundaries ... finally melting invisibly into the woods.

I remain still, savoring the unique feelings that accompany a close encounter with wildlife. Wonder. Blessing. Grace. A gift given.

The next time I see the deer, its fading spots have disappeared. Over several occasions, I learn its path through the woods. I learn to listen to the telltale delicate crunching of leaves and twigs as it makes its way. I learn to listen to the silence that sometimes whispers its presence.

Deer are one of the premier families of mammals, native to every continent except Australia. Stories and legends feature deer luring hunters or kings into the woods. Led astray, they are drawn into new adventures. Sir Gawain of King Arthur's Round Table had just such an encounter with a white stag.

In Native American beliefs, the deer embodies gentleness. In an interesting cross-cultural commonality, legend has it that the Buddha first preached in a deer park; he is often pictured with a deer, representing innocence and gentleness.

Gentleness and a call to new adventures. Rich notes in fall's song.

holy smokes, bullwinkle

When our notion of physical reality is violently interrupted, we are thrown into sheer terror. Nightmarish nanoseconds stretch timelessly, and the terror tears deep into the psyche.

My friend Tom was driving his Chevy Blazer, with me up front beside him. Out-of-town guests Pith and Shelly were in the backseat. Teddy-dog was all the way in the back. We were headed home, north on Route 91, after a delicious late dinner at the Colatina Exit. (Well, not Teddy. He waited in the car.)

Somewhere in those last miles before the Wells River exit, suddenly looming ahead in the headlights was . . . something. My boggled brain sent confused messages. *A man standing in the middle of 91? With the skinniest legs I've ever seen.* I yelled something inarticulate, and instinctively ducked.

The car swerved sharply, shoving me sideways. Then a violent, stunning impact, an explosive roar. The car swung. My brain sent a new message. *It is not possible to experience this and live.*

I rode a wave of waiting. For the end.

Suddenly, stillness and silence.

Then, Tom's voice. "Is everybody okay?" My first indication that life would go on.

Dazed, I slowly sat upright. Glass nuggets and pulverized glass powder slid down the back of my shirt. I turned to look in the backseat where Pith had his arm around Shelly. Everyone was in one piece, but Shelly had hit her head and had glass in her eyes. (Fortunately, her abrasions proved not to be sight-threatening. They healed quickly.)

The game warden estimated that the moose we'd hit weighed eight hundred pounds. It took two shots to put the poor thing out of its misery.

The next day, a full survey of the damage to Tom's car told the whole story. We were amazed and grateful for Tom's coolheaded driving. Forget those bumper stickers that say BRAKE FOR MOOSE AND LIVE. They should read, SWERVE FOR MOOSE AND LIVE.

Because Tom swerved, we hit the moose at an angle, so it was not tossed onto the roof. Its head and neck cleared the hood, then crushed the windshield in front of Tom and thudded down the driver's side—blowing out both windows, irreparably damaging those doors.

Counting blessings. The moose did not have antlers, which might have decapitated Tom. We were all wearing seat belts. Tom wasn't talking on a cell phone but had two hands on the wheel and all his attention on the road.

Gratitude. For all the emergency folks who showed up at the scene. Troopers Schulze, Potter, and Dudley who treated us with gentle kindness. The Woodsville ambulance crew—especially Gary Gagnon who turned his head like a gentleman, holding up a blanket, while I dropped my pants to unload glass that was working its way into delicate places.

Our cars give us an illusion of safe solidity. We forget how fast sixty-five miles an hour really is, how little time it gives us to react. We forget that wildlife is beyond our control.

Be careful. It's a jungle out there.

wild things

I live at the edge of wild woods. They embrace me from the north, south, and east. A beaver pond is across the road to the west. It's Grand Central to migrating ducks, geese, and creatures that trumpet strange noises in the night.

My ten acres melt into the acres of my neighbors, flowing all the way down from Blue Mountain into Ryegate Corner. In the twilight or under a full moon, coyotes commune. From someplace distant in the north to somewhere closer to the south, their frenzied yipping, barks, and howls echo.

It is a primal conversation, raising the hairs on the back of my neck. I alternate between standing mesmerized on my back porch and scurrying inside, unsettled by an ancient fear.

Teddy-dog knows the difference between these woods and those just beyond the house where we lived for so many years. There, he would dash down the path to the stream at the forest's edge at any time, ignoring my calls to come. Here, once dark has fallen, he acknowledges the hold of the wild on the woods.

When I let him out at night, Teddy first stands, stock-still, on the back porch. Raising his head, he tests the air, listening. Sometimes he growls, low in his throat, and will not leave the deck until I walk him down the steps.

Something is near.

In daylight, Teddy romps gleefully down the forest path. At

night, he does not stray beyond the line where the yard meets the trees. And even then, ears pricked, he does his business with dispatch, and dashes back to the porch.

Last fall, to celebrate the season, I bought three pumpkins. Small, medium, and large. I set them on the front-porch steps, in ascending order of size. One morning, I stepped outside to enjoy the bright but cool sunlight and beheld a very strange sight.

The smallest pumpkin had a nibble-sized bite taken out of it . . . The medium pumpkin had been sampled with a child's fist-sized bite . . . And the biggest pumpkin bore the wound of large jaws that took nearly half the vegetable's girth in a single chomp.

I felt like Goldilocks.

The front porch is very close to my bedroom window, but I hadn't heard a thing.

Teddy sniffed the pumpkins, then tracked the smell in agitation, snarling softly. It was a sound I had never heard from him.

There, in the morning light, I looked around furtively. As if whatever wild thing had done this might still be lurking nearby, poised to pounce . . .

Yielding to the creatures of the woods, I disposed of the pumpkins—hauling them far from the house.

This year, I bought six pumpkins. Miniature. Plastic. I hung them between the balusters of the front-porch railing. They glow neon in the twilight, pretty but benign. I will issue no invitations with fall decorations.

I live at the edge of the wild woods.

nothing wasted

I was on my way out to a dental appointment when I discovered a bird lying in my driveway. As I approached, I was especially distressed because at first glance I thought it was a hawk.

A bit over two years ago, during my first inspection of my present home, the real estate agent and I walked from the backyard into the woods. I looked up to see a hawk circling overhead. It was a special moment, and I've caught glimpses of that hawk (or so I fancy) ever since.

So when I saw the bird lying in my driveway, brown wings and white breast barred with brown, I thought it was my hawk.

On closer inspection, the straight, short beak convinced me it was not.

As I removed the still-limp body with a shovel, I saw no obvious injury. Recent headlines raised questions: bird flu? I wondered if I should call the game warden.

I stashed it under a laundry basket in the yard to deal with after the dentist. But on my way down the hill, I saw Bill Elder and Gene Perkins chatting outside the fire station. I told them about my mystery bird and asked if I should call the game warden.

"Sounds like a partridge," Bill said. "When we were kids, we used to hunt up there. It's all posted now. There're a lot of partridge. Cars flush 'em, they get hit."

But there were enough discrepancies in my description of the bird and Bill's knowledge to pique his curiosity. He jumped into his truck.

"I'll run up and take a look," he said, agreeing to call me later to let me know what it was. That evening, he confirmed that it was a young partridge.

"Did you put it out in the woods?" I asked.

"No-oo-oo," he said slowly.

"Put it back under the laundry basket?"

"Noo-oo-oo."

Bill was reluctant to tell me what he'd done. Something clicked.

"Did you take it home to eat?"

"Yup," he said, sprightly, sounding relieved.

"Oh, good," I told him. "Glad you felt you could."

There has been a growing gulf between hunters and non-hunters in recent years. More people—like me—have moved to the North Country from places where hunting is an alien culture. More land is posted, and families who have responsibly hunted local lands for generations feel a deep sense of loss. It is a loss that only those who have grown up in these woods can know.

Bill and I bridged that divide over the body of one young partridge. We went on to talk about deer, the burgeoning wild turkey population and its relationship to the increasing number of coyotes. I asked a bunch of wildlife questions and got knowledgeable answers.

Short of starvation, I will never shoulder a hunting rifle. But, more and more, I learn that hunting is about so much more than the kill.

strange november

This month has given us a gentle glide into winter, with record-setting warm temperatures and coatless after-noons.

On my way to a Christmas craft fair last week, I followed two motorcyclists down a sun-dappled road. Leaning artfully in and out of curves, their graceful, weaving dance was a rare mid-November sight.

Then rain and rain and rain saturated the ground. Mini-ponds pooled in hollows in the forest behind my house, bringing out the wood frogs from their hunkered-down hiding places. Their distinctive calls filled one balmy evening, joining with night birds' songs.

I swear I heard peepers. It sounded like spring.

The next day, a friend laughed that she'd gone outside that evening to realize it was warmer out in the night than it was in her house.

Twenty-four hours later, the forest ponds were rimmed with ice. A day after that, I was back on my front porch, basking in the afternoon sun.

As I sunbathed, I contemplated raking the leaves one more time. I noticed, too, that the lawn was furry with flourishing grass. Firing up the mower crossed my mind, but I dismissed the notion as too absurd for November.

Although I have not yet hauled out all my winter clothes and packed away the remnants of summer cotton, I have pulled out—piece by piece—coats and hats for frosty mornings. My closets are a testament to this strange November, with its spring wonders between raw moments of winter's first touch.

Thanksgiving snuck up on me. In this temperate November, I'm struggling to grasp the idea that Christmas is a mere month away. Still, some primal inner clock has me nesting for winter.

These days I rearrange rooms. I want to wash curtains. I'm redecorating the walls of my cave, where I will burrow in as cold winds sweep across the yard, sculpting the snow.

At some instinctual level, I am not fooled by this gentle November. My cells hold vivid awareness of winter's lassitude. I prepare my cave, set in provisions—knowing that swirling flakes will hypnotize me and drive me into cozy corners, desiring nothing more than a good book.

My mind may have trouble grasping the fact that Christmas is around the corner, but my body knows winter. It is not fooled by frogs.

winter dark mysteries

The first dusting of snow arrived with the full moon.

High on my hill in Ryegate Corner, there was just enough to sweep off the porches. Just enough to frost the trees and cover the dead brown detritus of fall.

After our strange November's warmth and rain, I welcomed the spindrift flurries' blessing. I am happy now for the transformation snow brings to the land, even though it heralds challenging months to come, and I know at the end I will yearn for green.

As darkness fell, the moon rose, bestowing otherworldly illumination. It was both eerie and peaceful. Blue-white light danced on pristine snow, casting bold tree silhouettes across my yard.

How could I resist the call to walk in the woods?

So bright was the night, Teddy-dog and I went without a flashlight. Only a few short yards down the trail into the forest and I was brought to a halt while Teddy romped ahead. It was the silence that stilled my steps.

There is nothing like the hush of the woods on a moonlit night after the first snow. More than mere quiet, it is an atmosphere. As if the trees had tucked themselves in for the long months ahead, but still whispered in the wind with a tidal song from the tops of their branches.

I sense hibernating critters hunkered down in burrows and

hollows. I feel their slow deep breathing resonate through the land.

I stand witness, mystified and wondering at the quietude, before following Teddy's cavorting paw prints. We make our way out to the point, where a circle of tall pines stands on the brink of gradually descending land.

We face the east. There, the mountains undulate in blue-gray, across the horizon. High above, the fat, full moon gleams. Teddy returns from snuffling along some creature's scented trail to sit by my side.

We stay, until the night wind penetrates our bones.

Hours later, as I sit in the kitchen sleepless with full moon and cradling a hopeful cup of warm milk laced with hot chocolate, a high-pitched scream splits the night.

So close, just beyond my door.

A chill of terror races down the back of my neck. The scream sounds human, like a woman's tormented shriek, but is followed by a low, growling gargle. An image leaps into my mind—that growl resonating from deep in a furry throat, emerging through fanged jaws clenched around some hapless critter.

Then the sounds stop as abruptly as they had pierced the quiet night.

I sweat with cold fear. Paralyzed.

Finally, I get up from my chair and peer out the window. The moonlit yard glows back at me. I see nothing between the shadows of the trees.

The wash of gentle moonlight hides night's dark mysteries.

winged friends

When I first moved to my new place, the air was empty . . .
The yard was quiet. There were no resident birds.

Oh, there were birds out in the woods. Birds flew high as
they passed by. Ravens conversed in the morning and crows
played tag.

But front yard and back, the trees were silent. It was an
eerie silence. Lacking life. As if I'd been dropped onto a bar-
ren planet.

There were always birds around my old house. I fed them
for years. I'm no expert, but I suspect that feeding opens up
the neighborhood—word gets out that here's a good place
to live. Local birds move in, and migratory throngs put your
place on their maps.

For the first month I was here, too much had to be done to
attend to the "get bird feeder" item on my list. I lived with the
discomfiting absence of birds.

Finally, things settled down and I took advantage of the generous gift certificate from my real estate agent, Dale Bromley.
Isn't it great fun to spend someone else's money? I splurged
at J&M Landscaping, buying a top-of-the-line tube feeder and
a wrought-iron pole that looks like a supersized shepherd's
crook.

Then I waited for the feathered flocks. And waited. And
waited.

Theoretically, I understand it takes a while for birds to find the seed. But here's the silly part . . . As the days passed, I felt rejected.

Every time I stood at the kitchen sink and saw the full, vacant feeder, I was bereft. I worried. Would I henceforth be living in bird-less loneliness?

One misty morning, the first wildlife visitor appeared. I should've figured. It was a big, fat, fluffy gray squirrel. Luxuriant fur and tail. By that time, I was so absurdly forlorn its presence cheered me.

A few hours later, I stepped to the sink. It took a few seconds for my brain to register what I saw. Every perch of the feeder was occupied.

Goldfinches sported their winter greenish gold hues. I caught my breath as they fed and flurried nervously. Goldfinches are skittish birds. When I moved just a hair, they fled en masse to the bare maple at the end of the yard.

But there they were. Up in the trees, scolding.

That was just the beginning. Soon the chickadees came. They are the teddy bears of birds, friendly and cuddly, unlike the fidgety finches. When the chickadees came, I knew I was home.

Here's my fanciful image. That gray squirrel went back out into the woods and announced the discovery of a safe feeding place.

Now my mornings are filled with birdsong. A sassy blue jay, complaining that the feeder perches are too small, is reduced to eating off the ground. Flocks of finches are startled into fleeing, then returning. Chickadees dart from feeder to trees in bobbing flight.

The air is filled with wings.

christmas stuff

I've been having interesting conversations with people about their Christmas gift preferences.

For myself, still settling into a smaller home, the very prospect of receiving any kind of stuff triggers a shuddering Grinch attack. Please. Nothing to unwrap, hold, or handle. Nothing to find a place for or to store.

Realizing that my attitude is prejudiced by weeks and weeks of sorting, giving away, selling, packing and unpacking, I wondered if my repugnance was simply situational. So I've been asking others . . .

How do you feel about getting stuff for Christmas?

My informal research indicates that the older a person is, the less they desire more possessions. Folks age fifty and up tend to feel they have enough stuff, and they're tired of taking care of what they have.

But generalizations are too . . . well, general. I've also talked with silver-haired citizens who joyfully collect dolls, china, trains, antique toys, et cetera, et cetera.

Thus, it isn't as simple as saying, "Well, Grandma's an old codger so she won't want any stuff."

The common advice is to ask someone what they'd like before you head off to shop. The problem is, many people will say one or more of the following: *"Oh, I have everything I*

need . . . I don't know; nothing in particular . . . Get what-
ever you think I'll like . . ."

Not helpful. The fumbling gift-giver is lost in limbo, wanting
to give something special but having no clue what that is. I'd
love to know how many Christmas shopping dollars are spent
on last-minute, desperate choices by frantic folks grabbing
any fool thing, hoping it will do.

Be kind. If you're asked what you'd like, give a constructive
answer. This includes the honest response, "I don't want any
thing."

Please note the emphasis. Just because someone doesn't
want stuff doesn't mean they don't want *anything*. I recently
talked with a woman who introduced me to a novel gift-giving
concept. She informed her family that she wants *experiences*
for Christmas.

"I gave my family a list of things I'd love to do . . . Go car-
oling, take a drive and see Christmas decorations . . . What I
really want is *time with them* doing fun things."

Some years ago, this woman decided she would not give
stuff as presents anymore. She gives gift certificates for mas-
sages, tickets to concerts—pleasures, not things.

I thought this was a great notion. What a rich approach.
What a perfect gift . . .

Unless, of course, you need to feed a collector's passion.

holiday tears and laughter

After the winds of change have blown through your life with hurricane force, holidays are especially difficult.

Fresh to a new home and a new life, I approached Christmas with trepidation and determination. Wisdom warned: It is folly to try to keep things the same when they are not at all the same.

Dancing with my own haunting shadows—struggling to find new ways to celebrate—I realized how many people were stumbling through similar steps in far more difficult circumstances. Across the North Country and the nation, there are empty places at the table. Beloved friends and family members are missing. Mothers and fathers, sons and daughters, sisters and brothers, aunts and uncles, childhood friends and co-workers are away—and in harm's way.

Some places at the table will remain empty.

Several dear friends are celebrating their first Christmas after the death of a loved one. Mother, father, husband . . . my friends are finding their way through tangled holiday trails in raw landscapes of loss.

The holidays are a tender time of traditions and memory. We hold our losses in our hearts, places we don't want to touch because they hurt. Sometimes I think the crazy commercialism and frenetic social whirl serve to distract us.

No one person can tell another how to dance their way

between shadows and light. For myself, I honor both tears and laughter. I don't expect a Norman Rockwell holiday of perfection. It's a relief not to measure what is against an idealized notion we feel compelled to fulfill.

For myself, I need to allow peace to enter my spirit. Even in the wake of emotional upheaval, this season offers joys and blessings, if we are open to receive them.

Shoveling the driveway at dusk the other day, I stopped to stretch my back. In a pristine moment, the hush of snow-laden pines in the waning light wrapped around me.

Shopping one afternoon, I bought tree lights. The clerk at Farmer Hodge's Christmas Shop offered to cut a hole in the bag. I was confused until she slipped the plug out and tested them to make sure they worked. I was moved, perhaps disproportionately, by her considerate gesture.

Friends' simple acts of thoughtfulness create memorable moments. We drive around looking at lights, tickled by yards transformed into carnivals of holiday fun.

For something new, I created a tree in miniature. It stands on a table in my window, sparkling light into the darkness. The tree would be at home in fairyland, and is—I hope—a treat for those driving by in these early-dark nights.

It is a tender time, this holiday season. May you dance it with grace.

birds' nests
and christmas trees

Since moving into my smaller house two years ago, I've downsized my Christmas trees. It wasn't a great sacrifice. I'd been leaning in that direction anyway.

As much as I love real trees, they are hard to manage when they're taller than I am. And given that I'm five foot two, most trees are.

My first year here, I had barely moved in when Christmas was upon me. Having no energy for a big fuss, I turned to what is charmingly referred to as a "tabletop tree." It wasn't easy to find, which surprised me. Many people live in small quarters and the North Country population is aging, so I thought alternatives to eight-foot trees would be readily available.

Last year, finding a little tree was even more difficult. And when I did, I was charged the price of a full-sized wonder. I questioned this and was told that, since the tree would someday be large if not taken earlier, the tree farmer had to be paid for its potential value.

It was the only tabletop tree I'd found. So I bit back the retort that by cutting the young tree, the farmer would not have to invest several more years of labor-intensive, careful pruning.

I wasn't happy, but I paid.

Later, I went with Tom to get his and his mother's tree from Ron and Joanne Fullerton. Their tree farm is in Newbury, but they sell trees and wreaths from their home on Swiftwater Road in Woodsville. I told them my sad tree tale, and they assured me that, in the future, they could provide me with a reasonably priced small tree.

So this year, I called the Fullertons. Ron cut a lush, small Fraser fir for me and charged half what I'd paid the previous year.

What a lovely Christmas gift. But there was more to come.

As Tom and I fitted the tree into its stand, I found a bird's nest nestled in the lower branches near the trunk. Three inches in diameter, it was tiny, perfect.

Enchanted, I delicately disengaged the nest, cradling it in the palm of my hand. We marveled at its woven artistry.

Tom said he'd heard that finding a bird's nest in a Christmas tree was good luck. I wondered about the origins of this concept and explored the Internet. After finding lots of websites that echoed the good-luck symbolism, I finally found something more specific from Sugar Pines Farm, an Ohio Christmas tree farm.

"A legend tells of the magic of all the world's birds bursting into song as if with one voice the night the Christ child was born. Your family may find a bird's nest in the Christmas tree—the gift of health, wealth and happiness throughout the year."

May your trees be filled with nests, and your holidays filled with joy.

a recipe for the new year

The end of the year invites contemplation.

In recent musings, I drifted into memories of kindnesses I've received throughout the year. Rather than making resolutions, I savored a year-end review of grace. Revisiting good deeds done for me felt so delicious, I realized I stumbled into a resolution after all.

To establish and sustain an attitude of gratitude.

I know the phrase is cliché. But I like its rhythmic poetry. And the truth is, there is as much power in gratitude as every minister, New Age guru, and life coach has repeatedly proclaimed.

Gratitude doesn't make your problems go away. It doesn't eliminate the host of evils romping through the world. But floating in its warm, golden waters is a balm to troubled minds and weary spirits.

Rising from even a quick dip into that pool, I am more peaceful. I am stronger. I can face the challenges besetting me with greater calm. There is more room in my spirit for empathy, less leaning toward judgment, more likelihood that I'll lend a hand where needed.

I am grateful to everyone who has enriched my days with simple, unselfish deeds—like my neighbor, Dottie Perkins.

Getting ready for a holiday party, I was feverishly baking my mother's brownies. (One of her enduring legacies is the best brownie recipe in the world.) I had melted the chocolate and butter, stirred in the flour, and was adding vanilla before mixing in sugar and eggs.

The recipe calls for two teaspoons of vanilla . . . and I came up exactly one-half teaspoon short. I know this precisely because I couldn't find my teaspoon measure and was using the half-teaspoon.

Here on my hill in Ryegate Corner, it's a good twenty-minute round trip to the store. So, between cursing and stamping my feet, I spun the Rolodex in my head for a neighbor who would be home and armed with vanilla.

Dottie was my second call. Not only did she have vanilla, she offered to bring it over.

"Oh, that's sweet of you," I said, "but it's my crisis, not yours."

"No, really," she said. "You're in the middle of baking. I'll be there."

And she was. She even sat down and had a cup of tea. On learning that I was baking my mother's brownies, she asked if Mom had baked much. The opportunity to talk about Mom was a special gift during the holidays, when we acutely miss our loved ones who have passed on.

How deeply pleasurable it was, positively primal. Two women chatting over tea in a kitchen redolent with something good baking in the oven. Dottie stayed long enough to have a brownie.

She left with Mom's recipe. And I was left with joy.

After this column appeared, many people asked for Mom's killer brownie recipe. So here it is, just as Mom wrote in the handwritten version I treasure—plus a couple of cooking hints from me.

"4 oz. unsweetened baking chocolate
2 sticks butter
2 cups sugar
4 eggs
2 teaspoons vanilla
1 cup flour
½ teaspoon salt
1 cup pecans, chopped

"Melt butter & chocolate over low heat in saucepan. Stir in other ingredients. It's not necessary to beat the batter. Bake in greased & floured pan at 350 degrees for 25–30 minutes.

"Note: After so many years of making these for your dad without nuts, I really prefer these brownies sans nuts. These keep very well in a covered container and freeze very well."

I swear, these are no more difficult to make than boxed mixes, and the results are a gourmet world away. Play with salt to taste. I completely forgot it one day and couldn't tell much difference, except they rose a bit better next time when I added ¼ teaspoon. The batter should be smooth like cake batter. Preheat the oven. Oil/flour spray-can products work fine for greasing the pan. Test brownies as you would cake; cooking times vary with ovens. Mom is right about their freezing well; defrost in microwave for a just-out-of-the-oven experience. They are so rich, I've never made them with nuts. The brownies will have an incredibly moist center, almost like fudge.

In memoriam, Nancy Jane Woody Flax
(and Seth Flax, who didn't like nuts in his brownies).

off the dish

I've cut the cord. This may not be the technically correct term, since I'm referring to the satellite dish that beamed a hundred-plus television stations into my home, but it feels metaphorically accurate.

I have severed the umbilical cord to the source of mother-media nourishment. And I'm doing just fine, thanks.

When I first moved to my new place, I had a trillion things to do. Reestablishing my dish connection wasn't at the top of the list. I was coping with minor details, such as the insurer canceling my homeowner's policy within weeks after I moved in.

Besides, my friend Dee—an invaluable, tireless workhorse—was staying with me during the transition. Hmmm, talk with a friend or watch TV? No contest.

Even before moving, I was ambivalent about the whole television thing. I'd been in front of the tube far too much and was looking for an excuse to change my ways. To top it off, my satellite company made a fiendish mess of canceling my service.

Their dish was gone, but they continued to bill me and inexplicably felt justified in doing so. It took a round robin of phone calls and about five hours to convince them this was unreasonable.

I wasn't inclined to do further business with them.

My new house came with a fancy antenna setup. ABC and Vermont Public Television come in sharp and clear, but CBS is

241

haunted with shadows, and it's always snowing on NBC. Each time I want to change stations, I have to get up and turn a dial to drive the antenna in the proper direction. This makes channel surfing a physical activity.

I admit I cheat. I have a friend with cable. He's very generous about taping special shows I see advertised but can't receive. However, it's also true that he has recorded more shows than I've gotten around to watching.

Here are some of the dish-less joys I've discovered . . .

My evenings are no longer divided into half-hour or hour slots when I'm watching or waiting to watch something. I'm not carrying television schedules around in my head. (Okay, except for *West Wing.*) I watch a lot of public television. Vermont's version is much higher quality than the national feed I received via the dish.

I take moonlight walks into the woods. I listen to more music than I have in years. And sometimes, I just sit in the silence.

The first time I was up late and WCAX *went off the air*, I was stunned. After so many years on the satellite, I'd forgotten that broadcast stations actually stop broadcasting. I felt as if I were in a time warp, back in the days before round-the-clock television.

"WCAX now ends its broadcast day. Good night."

Indeed. I turned off the set and went to sleep.

heave-ho

I have a new hobby and a new exercise regime. They are, in fact, the same activity—pushing snow, wrestling with ice.

My new home has a long, broad blacktop driveway. The single-story house has a metal roof, perfectly poised over front and back porches. It's only mid-January. I've already lost track of how many complete roof loads of snow I've cleared away.

The upside is that I'm developing a six-pack of abdominal muscles where there once was a modest midriff bulge. While brushing my hair the other day, I was surprised by biceps flexing merrily in the mirror. Mine.

The downside is that I ache in places continually introducing themselves to me . . . and I'm becoming obsessed. Or perhaps I'm becoming addicted.

You've read about runner's high? Endorphins—otherwise known as "happy hormones"—are released in the brain with sustained running. Some runners confess the high is what drives them out to pound the pavement.

They need their fix. Admittedly, there are worse monkeys to have on your back. But it's strange to feel restless and irritable when the shovel is not in my hands. Never mind the dishes piled up in the kitchen, or the bills piled elsewhere . . . I gotta get out there.

There's an art and intimacy to this snow management business. I've come to know every dip and curve of pathway and driveway. Which angle of shoveling is best here, which is better there.

Dancing with snow involves delicate timing. I've learned to wait until the temperature is just right. Then I can dislodge a frozen mound of snow from the front porch and slide its glacial mass off the corner by the steps.

Strategic planning is also called for. Wait until the roof has served its full offering, or shovel in increments? It depends on how abundant the load is, and when the temperature shifts. Fluffy, cold snow is light, presenting a whimsical workout. Add a little warmth, and the snow is heavily wet.

And, always, I am aware of my limitations. Aware of the toll of repeated motions. So I play with positions. Switching the shovel to my non-dominant left hand. Consciously avoiding the twist-and-toss motion my chiropractor warns against. With monster shovelfuls, I squat, shift my hands as if holding a barbell, and lift, mimicking beefy weightlifters going for gold.

I've failed, many times, to keep to an exercise routine. Even ten minutes a day, every day, seems an impossibility. I admire people who exercise regularly, disciplining themselves for the benefits it brings.

Exercise for its own sake just bores me to tears.

But, oh, dump me some snow . . . and let me survey the landscape cleared by my own sweat. Then I really feel I've *done* something. No delayed gratification. No theoretical, far-off benefits. The blacktop shines in the sun. The planks of the porches greet me with woody clarity.

Then the snow begins to fall again.

magic morning

This unseasonable warmth has been unsettling. As much as we might complain about North Country cold, it is the natural order here. And though we may delight in the luxurious lack of frigid temperatures and stormy days, it is unsettling when a winter's spring goes on too long.

I know I'm not the only one whose sleeping patterns have been disturbed.

Winter sleep is different. Snuggled under cozy covers or rendered dopey by the woodstove, our days end earlier than in bright, warm months. We sleep lightly in spring, when morning birdsong is still new and wakes us before our appointed hour. While we may not actually hibernate, sleep is deeper in winter, and we are often loath to leave our beds.

But this winter, my hibernation response has been disrupted. So when I came fully awake one recent morning to that strange blue-gray light of predawn, I was not surprised.

This light is like no other—reminiscent of old, fine-art photos or Chinese ink paintings in subtle-hued gradations, imbuing simple black and white with richness and depth.

It doesn't last long. Whether skies are clear or overcast, sunrise changes the light. Predawn slips away. The snow once again gleams white. The green of pine and spruce asserts itself. Shadows shift from a slate radiance to simple shade. The sky loses luminescence.

On this wakeful morning, while predawn magic held, I was drawn outside.

Standing on my back porch, I savored the ephemeral light. I breathed in cold, crisp air while beholding snow-crested pines. Through dense woods, between trunks and branches, I discerned the stain of sunrise spreading above mountains.

I heard a cautious crunch of snow and felt the unseen presence of something wild. I stood still, eyes searching the tree line. Nothing. I remained still.

A deer charged up the bank, out of the ravine where water flows. Powerful haunches drove hooves briefly noisy on the crusty snow and he was gone, a silent shadow between trees. Then I heard again the cautious crunch as he moved deeper into the woods.

It was as if we had a date, that deer and I—fleeting moments intense with accidental beauty.

I stood awhile, listening to the fading echo of hooves. Sunrise set distant mountaintops aflame.

Later that morning, I came to this line in an Elizabeth Berg novel: "This is my true religion: arbitrary moments of nearly painful happiness for a life I feel privileged to lead . . ."

Oh, yes.

teddy and the turkeys

It's amazing what a difference a quarter of a mile makes. That's approximately the distance between my former home and my present one.

Up here, higher on the hill, the woods are wilder. The ten acres behind my house stretch into pastureland and forest ranging from Ryegate Corner up Blue Mountain. That's a good chunk of natural habitat, only sparsely dotted with human presence.

There are lots of critters out there in the woods. On still mornings and in the quietude of dusk, I hear secretive rustlings. The snow bears witness to resident creatures whose tracks I cannot yet decipher.

There are nights when the coyotes' howling sends eerie chills down my spine. I heard them at the old place, but their wails echoed from a distance. Now they're so close, the vibration of their yowling reaches into that visceral place where man and beast have always been natural adversaries.

I don't let Teddy go into the woods at night. He would be a morsel, a delicacy for the wild things.

Teddy weighs maybe twenty pounds. My vet's best guess is that he's a cross between a poodle and a silky terrier. I chose his name because he resembles a cuddly blond teddy bear.

Like many small dogs, Teddy thinks he's a lion. He has threatened horses and cows. With fierce abandon, he rushes in where angels fear to tread. He'd take on a coyote without quivering a whisker.

Teddy loves to romp in the woods. In deference to his lack of judgment, I walk with him or keep him in sight, even in daylight. There are always surprises in the forest.

Just beyond my yard, the land rises slightly, then slopes steeply down. That natural trough is hidden from view, though the path Teddy runs on the other side is within sight. One morning, I stood on the deck watching him scamper joyfully along that ridge. Neither of us saw the turkeys silently trekking through the trough.

Suddenly there were panicked turkeys everywhere. As they desperately tried to take flight, the thrump of their wings sounded like slow helicopter blades. Lots of helicopters, mere yards away. A half dozen birds broke left, another half dozen broke right, and in the middle stood a stunned Teddy.

Even from a distance, I could see his expression change from "What's this?" to "Oh, what fun!" In a split second, Teddy launched into action, scattering turkeys with blissful abandon.

I couldn't count them. I can't possibly describe the cries they made. But that sound of wings—*thrump, thrump*—drummed on. All around were turkeys trying to lift their heavy bodies, dodging branches, crashing through brush, scurrying over the snow.

They kept coming and running and flying from different directions. Teddy was bedazzled. He simply sat down and watched.

Then, when they'd all disappeared, Teddy ran back to me with pride and glee.

It was a good morning.

what works

The big storm left a prodigious amount of snow to be shoveled, pushed and wrestled from one place to another. A week later, I was still at it.

The task must be undertaken in steady stages, particularly if one is not blessed with a snowblower. Especially when one resides at the halfway point between the fifth and sixth decades of life.

Tom came over to help. In the absence of a snowblower, a strapping, nearly inexhaustible man is a darn good second. His height and strength are indispensable. The snow on the sunny side of the house slid from the roof onto the front deck. I would have been standing mid-torso in snow and chunks of ice had I attempted to clear it.

Not that I didn't do my fair share. It took more than an hour to clear the barricade in front of the garage door. Thanks to the plow guy and the wind, there was a hip-high wall to be dismantled.

Among my many clearing tasks, I had animal accommodations to make. Teddy-dog stands less than two feet high. In the deep, fluffy snow, his attempts to get to the woods and do his business resembled a dog paddling to keep its head above water. Impossible to lift a leg under such circumstances.

A few years ago, I realized that making a path to the fuel tanks was much more manageable on snowshoes than with a shovel. Easier on the back, and the chore feels more like play. The same technique works for making dog paths to Teddy's favorite trees.

Tromp, tromp . . . and soon there's a nicely packed trail. Given the depth of the snow, they must seem more like tunnels than trails to Teddy.

Stomping paths creates space for the mind to meander. Somewhere in the midst of snow labors, it sank in that, despite the severity of the storm, I had never lost power.

My pre-storm preparations were focused on the near-certainty that, at some point, I would lose electricity. Up here on the hill in Ryegate Corner, that happens with all kinds of inclement weather. In recent years, it has seemed to occur more frequently and for longer periods.

But in this monster storm, nary a flicker.

This got me thinking about how quickly we respond when something doesn't work. I'm immediately on the phone to Green Mountain Power when the electricity goes off. Local and national news headline power outages, reporting how many hundreds of customers are suffering.

I have never heard a report like this: "Despite a fierce winter storm, thousands of customers received uninterrupted power. Kept warm in their homes, with the benefit of running water (and flushing toilets), people rode out the nor'easter in comfort."

Wouldn't the folks at the power companies be surprised if they received a flood of grateful phone calls?

We have to take action when things don't work. But it would be darn good for us all to celebrate when they do.

bug buddies

I am in the company of ladybugs.

This morning, I spot one meandering around the edge of the cup that holds my toothbrush.

A ladybug greets me from her trek across the kitchen counter as I make a sandwich. One nestles on the plate where my tea bags drain, a companionable presence as I brew my second cup of the day. In the evening, reaching for a towel, I encounter another exploring the folds.

At the old house where I once lived, winter ladybugs congregated by the dozens inside south-facing window frames. But here, I've only seen solitary bugs.

I wondered then, and now—what do they eat, how to they sustain themselves in my home? I admit that sometimes I've carefully transferred them from the unnatural wastelands of counters or rugs to a houseplant. But they don't stay among the leafy greens.

My curiosity sent me zooming into cyberspace.

Ladybugs, it turns out, are attracted to light-colored houses, like mine. They especially like older buildings with lots of cracks and crevices. The space behind clapboards is a favorite place for winter nestling.

They begin moving in during the fall, attracted by the heat our homes emit. Like most of us at this time of year, they prefer sunnier, warmer locales. Thus, they gravitate toward the south and southwest sides of buildings.

I didn't find an explanation for what wakes them up and brings them into our rooms. But I did discover that, once they've found a good place to hang out, they tell all their friends and relatives. Kind of like an AAA guide to the best hotels.

I'm not joking. Ladybugs release pheromones, a sort of buggy "perfume" that attracts other ladybugs. The scent is detectable up to a quarter of a mile away. Can you imagine? And it remains year after year, advertising a good place to winter over.

While hibernating, ladybugs live off their own body fats. (Wouldn't we just love that! How thin we'd be by spring.)

But coming inside can spell their doom. Ladybugs need humidity. In our heat-dry houses, they die of dehydration. That explains why my ladybugs hang out by tea bags and toothbrush, drinking water and other fluids.

Innumerable people complain on the Internet about severe ladybug infestations. In large amounts, ladybug perfume is apparently pretty stinky. Complaining homeowners insist that ladybugs *bite*. Strategies for banishing the little critters are shared and evaluated.

For me, though, the occasional ladybug simply slows me down. I don't fancy ingesting one with my morning tea or running one across my teeth. My gentle vigilance makes me more conscious of my surroundings.

There is a gift in this. I revel in details I would not notice if I were I dashing to and fro. The kiss of sun rays on the leaves of the ficus by my door. Crystal-cast rainbows dancing on my ceiling . . .

There is a gift in this.

the big snow

It was a dark and stormy night.

Okay, this is one the most recognized clichés in the English language. Beyond the hallowed halls of literature, the phrase was immortalized in its triteness by Snoopy. Perched atop his doghouse with his typewriter, the beagle plugged away at his Great American Novel, never getting much beyond this hackneyed adage.

I don't care.

It was dark. It was stormy. It was night . . . and it was magnificent.

Snow had been falling all day, and it just kept coming. It was so fine the air was veiled in mist. Like the airy spray from a waterfall, which is surprisingly drenching, the swirling veils of snow layered a thick blanket over everything by evening.

Then the winds came.

I turned on the outside lights to watch the show. Snow blew sideways. Snow spiraled like smoke, glittering hypnotically. It was impossible to tell what was coming from the sky, what was blowing off the roof, what was being lifted from the ground. Gusts swept curtains of snow across the window so I couldn't even see the railings of my front porch.

It was the first whiteout I've experienced while sitting comfortably in my living room.

When there was a lull in the whipping winds, I looked out

on a transformed landscape. Snowbanks undulating like sand dunes, as if sculpted by tender caresses. Every ridge and rough edge softened, curved, frozen in place.

A desert of snow.

The curves called to me. I wanted to walk in that strangely desolate, beautiful world.

By the time I'd layered against the cold, the gusts had begun again. Stepping outside, I felt a thrill of elation in the winter wildness. I walked in nature's paradox. In a world of sleek contours and serene surfaces frosted to perfection, sharp, whipping winds and stinging fragments burned my face.

In pools of illumination cast from my house, the play of light and shadow revealed the ebb and flow of snow, striations etched like geologic markers in stony canyon walls. As I walked, the surface cracked with each step, releasing puffs of snow in small explosions. The powder, lifted by the wind, eddied up my body and bathed my face.

I cannot fully convey my experience of nature's madcap romp. Something primal is at play. A wildness in the human spirit rises to dance with the pines, to the sibilant, symphonic accompaniment of the wind.

I am awed by such power and grandeur . . . yet there is also a sense of nature meeting nature, spiraling from within and without, a helix spinning.

When words fail, we stumble on clichés . . . It was a dark and stormy night.

And it was magnificent.

fire and ice

High winds a few weeks ago brought down three towering evergreens on my land. More precisely, they fell across the frozen vernal pond south of my front yard.

Since weather forecasters were predicting warm temperatures, I figured those fallen giants needed to be dealt with pretty quickly. Once the ice melted, I'd really have a mess. So that weekend, Tom fired up my chain saw.

There were lots of dead branches, and he planned to build a fire, burning them as he went along. "Won't the fire burn through the ice and just sink the whole thing?" I asked.

Tom grinned. "Dunno. I've never done this before."

I was recovering from a cold and had some pressing paperwork to attend to, so Tom worked solo for some hours . . . until the late afternoon when bright sunshine was too powerful a siren call for me to resist.

It was a magical sight. First, I beheld the fire's remains glowing at the east end of the pond. "It didn't burn through!" I called out to Tom.

"Nope," he replied, hauling a bunch of green branches into the woods.

The denuded tree trunks bisected the west end, and the pond was rimmed by a ring of snow. Tom had begun to create an ice rink.

"It'll be perfect," he said, heedless of winter leaning toward spring.

While he shoveled, I fed dead branches to the embers until the fire flamed high into the descending dark. And then the coyotes began to howl.

Tom and I stood by the fire in the primal dark. "I feel like I'm in a horror movie," I whispered.

"Don't go into the woods," he intoned with dire emphasis.

The next day, Tom cut up the tree trunks, and the circle of ice lay clean and whole within the circle of trees surrounding the pond. It was beautiful.

"Do you suppose now that you've built it, they will come?" I joked. "Ghostly hockey players in the night?"

I haven't heard the thwock of sticks and puck out there. But two fifty-something fools frolicked on the ice with as much abandon as their bodies would allow. You'd have to count by decades the number of years it had been since either of us was last on skates.

By moonlight and Coleman lantern, we wobbled our way around the rink the day after Town Meeting. It was far from an Olympic performance, but neither of us ended up on our keisters.

The weather forecasters say we're in for some warming, some rain, then back to colder temperatures. The ice just might be perfect. Again.

spring slide

I welcome the shift to spring, but the brown of *between*—before the green—is wearisome.

Just days before the spring equinox, there was enough snow to blanket my yard. At this time of year, a light layer of snow makes me downright cheerful. It won't amount to much, it won't last long, and the weight of winter is behind us.

My chickadees and nuthatches fed casually during warmer days. I imagined they were happy foraging out in the woods, flitting gaily through the defrosting countryside. But the flurry of snow brought them back in force . . .

. . . along with the red squirrels.

Not by choice, I've been supporting a small colony of squirrels through winter. A single pair became a quartet, then a sextet. When they feed from the ground beneath the feeder, I am good-natured about their presence. But one bold little bugger figured out that he could stand on the corner of the deck, leap sideways onto the wrought-iron shepherd's crook, and shimmy up to gain purchase on the feeder.

There he'd stay, scarfing down prodigious amounts of seed, until I indignantly burst out the back door to chase him away. I've been playing this non-contact game of tag throughout the morning for several days.

All because I ran out of Vaseline.

Last year, I learned the trick of spreading the gooey stuff on the feeder pole. You can spend a small fortune on "squirrel-proof" feeders (and I have), but nothing is as effective as this simple trick. Assuming you have no branches nearby from which the critters can launch themselves onto a feeder, this is an inexpensive squirrel defeater.

And it's cheap entertainment, too. Ever seen a squirrel sliding down a pole?

The first time I applied the goop, I went overboard. I was so determined to conquer the insatiable creatures that I coated the pole all the way from the ground up and over the curve of the shepherd's crook.

I had forgotten that birds like to perch at the top of the crook before dropping down to feed . . . I watched, helpless with laughter and guilt, as a chickadee alighted there and slid—upright and sideways—down the pole. I had terrible visions of birds sliding off tree branches throughout the woods . . .

How could a bird clean Vaseline off its feet?

Last week—as I kept watch on that snowy, nearly spring morning for the return of my tag teammate—a bright splash of color caught my eye. Between the two pine trees, hopping along on the ground, was one fat, saucy robin. Against the whitened yard, its red-orange breast was clarion.

The sight thrilled me. In that moment, with the robin, spring became more than a date on the calendar.

It became a bright flame in my spirit.

snail mail and other pleasures

The other day, I had one of those slap-in-the-face experiences. A confrontation between *now* and *then*. We all have such moments. Sometimes sad, sometimes nostalgic, always surprising—we see the landscape of our lives anew.

I received an envelope in the mail from my friend Nils out in California. Enclosed were newspaper articles in which he'd been mentioned, fifteen minutes of fame he'd spoken of in our frequent email exchanges. With the clippings, he enclosed a short letter, his flowing script detailing outcomes of the unexpected publicity.

Standing in my kitchen, staring at his blue-penned lines dancing across white paper, suddenly I could not read the words. His penmanship entranced me. It was as if I beheld a long-lost friend, unexpectedly returned. I was swept up in sweet reunion.

Before computers, Internet, and email, we kept in touch with letters. Back then, my friend and I exchanged pages and pages of handwritten thoughts, stuffed thick in envelopes that delighted with their weight even before the seal was broken.

Later, when our lives became busy, we sent typewritten letters, but there were always several lines scrawled at the end.

But with the ease and instant gratification of email, his

script was lost to me. Savoring the pleasures of swift electronic messages, I had not realized what a significant loss this was until I held in my hands the page he had penned, and felt reunited with an absent and dearly beloved friend.

I rarely get letters anymore. I keep in touch with far-flung friends and family by computer. Email is a blessing. It's so easy to share ordinary events that wouldn't be worth the effort of a letter. Distant relationships thrive through electronically sharing such unremarkable details of our daily lives, but we pay a price for this gift.

Going to the mailbox has lost that old edge of suspenseful delight. I no longer wonder who might have sent me a letter; I simply collect the junk mail and bills.

In places where I keep treasures, there are bundles of letters stored with loving care. Letters from my father, letters from my mother became especially precious after they died.

When I ache with homesickness for my folks, I open the cedar chest and take out the pages filled with their distinctive scrawls. Dad was left-handed and printed in spiky jolts as bold as his mind. Mom's cursive was a cussed challenge, as complex as the woman herself.

There is no intimacy on the computer screen, no warmth in laser-printed text. I am glad to have penned pieces of my past, artifacts from days gone by.

Every stroke and dot drawn by their hands evokes the lingering warmth of their touch.

feathered frenzies

As one storm moved in after another, the bird population at my feeder grew exponentially.

An entire flock of purple finches joined the yellow finches already residing in the woods near the house. The jaunty juncos patrolled the ground beneath the feeder, increasing their search in widening circles as more troops arrived.

Sparrows must have sent out a call to their brethren. With bird book in hand, I identified varieties I had never seen before.

My regular crew of chickadees, nuthatches, and blue jays was overwhelmed by the invasion. Finches are particularly ill mannered. They fight among themselves to hold feeding perches and snipe at one another even on the ground. Chickadees and nuthatches won't stand up to them and are driven away. Sparrows are more individual in their responses; some stand their ground, others flee.

The jays are too big for the feeder, which doesn't keep them from making the occasional attempt. They are big and plump, with rough reputations, but even they back down from the finches' aggression.

Finches are jittery creatures. If I move suddenly at the kitchen window, they are startled into flight en masse. Abandoning feeder and the rich pickings below, they retreat into the trees, watching and waiting until they deem it safe to return.

The politely patient chickadees and nuthatches take advantage of the fighting finches' withdrawal. Swooping from trees near and far, they snatch a single seed, fly off to feed, and repeat this process until the finches reclaim dominance.

I swear, Teddy-dog figured out these feathered feeding patterns and decided to even the odds. All the birds have become accustomed to his sphinx-like presence on the deck near the feeder. For days, I watched a silent Teddy watch the birds. One afternoon, when the finches had held reign for quite some time, Teddy suddenly barked sharply. Just once.

The finches took harried flight, joined by juncos. The nuthatches and chickadees moved in, bobbing to and fro. After a while, the finches returned. Teddy allowed them to gather in large numbers, squabbling among themselves, jockeying to keep perches they'd claimed, feeding greedily.

Then, he barked again. The finches took panicked flight in a flurry of full-flock wings. The pacifist population returned.

I nearly dropped the dish I was washing, I shook so hard with laughter.

As he played on, there was no mistaking Teddy's game for coincidence. At some point, the juncos got the idea and stopped fleeing with the finches.

Of course, I cannot know for sure that Teddy is truly benevolent in his sport. Perhaps he simply enjoys the riot of wings his single bark incites.

I cannot know for sure. But undeniably, the peaceful birds, the little guys, get more time at the feeder when Teddy takes his post.

So call it a flight of fancy, or call it anthropomorphizing, call it what you will. I believe Teddy roots for the feathered underdogs and has appointed himself their champion.

invisible ducks

T he real estate listing for this house and land described a "woodland setting with a small pond." But when I first visited in late summer, I did not see a pond.

I asked the owner about it. Peter pointed to what appeared to be a meadow in a hollow below the hill.

"There," he said.

With nary a drop of water to be seen, I looked at him quizzically.

"When the snow melts, that fills up. Usually, it stays full at least into summer. This is the first year it has dried up," he explained.

I nodded vaguely, thinking cynically about real estate sales. "An ocean view" from an apartment where you'd have to stand on the toilet and peer through the upper corner of a window . . . a puddle that becomes "a pond."

"And in the spring," Peter continued, "ducks come to it. You'll hear them, lots of them, but you'll never see them." He shrugged, indicating the mysterious nature of the ducks.

Uh-huh. I loved the place and bought it anyway, phantom pond notwithstanding.

Sure enough, when winter's snow melted, a wide waterway flowed down through the woods behind my house, filling the area Peter had indicated. And sure enough, when the weather warmed, I heard the ducks.

At first, there were just a few. I never saw them come, I never saw them go. Soon, especially in early morning and evening, there was a cacophony of quacking.

I wanted to see the ducks. I approached the pond from every direction. From the road. From the woods. From my front yard. No matter which way I came, they fell silent—and when I reached the pond, there was nothing but water to be seen. Not a feather in sight.

I tried spying with binoculars. Still nothing.

When Tom came to visit, he also became intrigued by the ducks-that-would-not-be-seen. How they could be so loud, then melt into the woods so perfectly? It was baffling. He called them chameleon ducks.

We lay in wait silently, hidden by small pines. Nothing.

Daily, their numbers multiplied—symphonies of quacking . . . and I became suspicious. How could *that many ducks* not make a sound on the dry-leafed woods floor, when I could hear a robin's footsteps? How could I not hear a wing beat?

When the peepers also began to sing their night and morning songs, I made a leap . . .

My research confirmed it. *Rana sylvatica.* Wood frogs. Found in forests and woodlands, they breed in vernal pools. These frogs "freeze" during winter, emerge quickly from hibernation, and travel to their breeding pools.

Their mating call is, and I quote from Library ThinkQuest, "a 'quacking' sound that is often confused with a duck's call."

Now, if you knew about wood frogs, you're probably having a good laugh on us for all those days Tom and I spent stalking ducks-that-were-not-ducks. But I had never heard a frog quacking . . .

Or maybe I had, and just thought it was a duck.

nature's mentors

Every life is a journey without completion.

I wish someone—anyone—had told me that when I was growing up. Don't you? If they had, I'd be a more peaceful person now.

Instead, we grow up in a world that feeds us the frustrating illusion that arrival is just around the corner. With the next achievement . . . But when we get there, the bar has been moved. There is a new set of standards to be met. And we begin the chase again.

I'm sitting on my back porch as I often do these days, watching nature struggle from winter into spring. Observing the agonizingly slow transformation of trees from skeletal hibernation into leafy lushness. I am so ready for full green.

How lucky the trees are. They do not engage in self-evaluation and critical judgment of their own performance—the rate at which they sprout buds, how long it takes for those pregnant pods to open.

Nature does not question its own nature. I believe that somewhere, somehow, deep in sentient sap, trees know this spring crawl is simply one cycle—and they are unconcerned. They will be bare again, and leafed again, and gloriously, outrageously colorful again before every leaf dies and falls away . . . leaving them bare to the bones, outlined in snow, frozen in ice, as the cycles turn.

There are no beauty contests for trees.

No report cards.

No quarterly job performance evaluations.

Trees stand. They sway in the wind, storms steal their branches. Sometimes they are scored by lightning. Bearing the scars, the trees' remaining branches still dance through the cycles, flowering into fullness.

It takes a long time for a tree to die.

And as it moves toward death, still it supports life. Insects move in through broken bark, woodpeckers mine the buggy gold. Eventually, the tree falls. Coming to rest on the forest floor, it invites mosses and offers softening wood to small critters burrowing into safe havens. Decaying, it becomes a composting cauldron of nutrients feeding the earth.

No one says to the tree in deprecating tones, "My, you're awfully slow to produce leaves!"

No one says, "What? Still *there*? Just lying around, stuck in the same place?"

And if they did, the tree wouldn't care.

Trees abide by their own rhythms. For them, one turn of the cycle is no better than the next. (Is that why they chatter so happily in the breeze?) Their glorious leafing is exuberantly unself-conscious. In dormancy, they rest without regret. Without self- recrimination.

Oh, to be a tree.

towels and other complaints

Here's an idle observation that turned into a "those were the days" cranky contemplation.

When did high quality become synonymous with *luxury*?

Towels brought this complaint to the fore. I've noticed that new towels I've bought just do not hold up. Sometimes after the first washing, sometimes after a few, the pathetic things simply begin to lose it. They shed linty detritus. The little loops of their weave unloop. Heaven forbid that you catch a loop on a fingernail. It'll pull the whole thread out of line.

This assumes you have been lucky enough to find a towel you're tempted to buy in the first place. Most new, reasonably priced towels have all the thick fluffiness of a cat's tongue.

You have to be willing to spend the equivalent of a linen-tablecloth dinner for two on a single bath towel to find one that will make you sigh with pleasure. When did that happen?

I have towels my mother passed down to me at least twenty years ago. (She died more than a decade ago, and heaven knows how many years she'd used them before I got them.) They're still softly thick and thirsty. The most wear some show is a raggedy edge here and there. Nothing a turn at the sewing machine couldn't fix.

I guarantee you there's not a designer label in the bunch. They were just ordinary, buy-'em-anywhere towels.

My grandmother, bless her soul, passed down to my mother some lovely hand-embroidered pillowcases. (If you're lucky, you can find their kind at antiques shops.) I have them now. The years have worn the cotton to a silky softness that meets your cheek like a good-night kiss.

I'm sure my grandmother never heard the phrase "thread count."

If you're Oprah Winfrey, you can spend well into triple digits for a zillion-thread-count set of sheets that'll make you feel like a queen. My grandparents didn't pay a premium for the privilege.

When I moved to the North Country in the late '70s, my parents began giving me flannel sheets for Christmas. They're finally just wearing out. I'm looking to replace them. But new ones don't have the warm fuzziness of my old ones, holey as they are.

And don't get me started on furniture. Oh, for the days when wood was *wood*. When craftsmanship was standard, rather than being created only as a specialty by exclusive artisans.

The conventional wisdom is that you get what you pay for. Well, maybe so. But what you get now is much less than it used to be. And that's not just due to inflation.

It's because high quality has become synonymous with luxury and only comes at a premium price.

april snow

Just when we felt spring was only one warm breeze away, an early-April winter storm blew in. The snow was heavy and wet.

Falling, it looked like miniature snowballs thickening the air. The day before, I had noticed tiny buds on the maple trees. Now each bare branch and twig was again etched in white. A classic New England Christmas card vision.

I ventured out that snowy day to the town clerk's office on my annual spring pilgrimage to renew Teddy's dog license. Everyone was talking about the weather.

"Looks more like December than December did," Marsha Nelson observed with good-natured acceptance.

Others have not been so sanguine about stepping back into winter. I will refrain from quoting them. That kind of language doesn't belong in our newspaper.

But the truth is, we generally have at least one last-bash snow in April. As seductive as the early warm days are, I've learned to enjoy each one but contain my enthusiasm while we dangle on the brink of spring.

The sunny weekend before the storm, I talked with a friend in Burlington who was puttering happily in his garden. Uncovering the green shoots just breaking ground, he gloried in seeing his plants emerge. I envied him those earthy smells and sights. My desire to get outside flared compellingly.

But I would hold out against my drive to play in the dirt. I knew from years past there would be white April showers, and the thought of exposing tender new growth to the inevitable strengthened my determination.

I blush to admit the storm also sparked a certain sentimentality . . . It was time to bid an affectionate farewell to another winter.

As much as I have basked in the warmth of early spring, I regret the passing of winter's quiet time. That cathedral hush of the woods after a fresh, heavy snowfall. Snow-crystal rainbow diamonds glistening in the sun. The cozy peace of my home as winter winds howl.

Soon, the frenzy of spring will be in full swing. The riot of renewed growth will fuel our energies, propelling us toward outside chores and joys. Friends and neighbors will emerge from winter's cocooning, and social calendars will bloom.

Wasps will return to the eaves around my porch. Blackflies will take their bite out of the loveliest of long-awaited balmy days. Mosquitoes will claim early summer.

But my flowering trees will dress themselves in glory. Wild blackberries will tempt me to dance among thorns. I will feel the sun's heat soak down to my bones and will reacquaint myself with my body, unencumbered by bulky clothing. I will delight in the cool kiss of water on my skin, swimming on a hot summer day.

Each season brings its own wonders and joys. Each bears its own burdens.

This is the magic of life in the North Country.

tending the land

These are the glorious early days of spring, before the blackfly invasion. It's a perfect time for outside work, especially in the woods.

Just beyond my backyard, the forest encircles my home. An old narrow logging road winds out into the woods, thick with pine and spruce and fir. There is very little hardwood old growth—that was logged out not so many years ago. In its absence are riots of young trees. White birch, yellow birch, soft maple, but also poplar and other junky growth.

My small homestead is on a high hill above Ryegate Corner. At the end of one of the forest trails is what I call The Point— a beautiful place where the land plateaus, then descends. The slopes were nearly clear-cut and are crowded with saplings. Leafed out, they create a wall through which one can only peek. In the distance, mountains outline the eastern horizon.

It is a fearsome thing to take down a tree. Any tree. But I have learned that the woods benefit from wise management. Spruce will flourish with outspread branches if not crowded by other trees. Birch blossoms when it doesn't have to compete with poplar for earth's nutrients.

When your goal is to cut selectively—to improve the health of the forest and gain a few windows on a distant view—you need a logger who shares your feelings for the land. Someone who considers what is best for each tree, and for each neighboring tree. Someone who shares your values and your vision.

This may sound awfully touchy-feely for guys who wield chain saws and take tractors onto the land. But trust me when I tell you that beneath their brawn, some of our local loggers have an abiding appreciation and respect for the woods.

I've been fortunate to work with two such men. Gene Zambon worked with me on the woods at my old home, and Darryl Perkins helps me now—teaching me forest husbandry.

The lay of the land is such that, even if I took down every tree from my backyard all the way out to The Point, I would not have a panoramic mountain view. But from my deck I can catch glimpses of mountaintops through the trees.

After only two days, Darryl's labor has changed the landscape. There is a remarkable magic as the contours of the land are revealed. Sometimes, the removal of a single tree opens a line of sight I couldn't have imagined.

From my back deck, I now see more deeply into the woods. Humps and hillocks undulate, ravines dip. A mountaintop greets me. Out at The Point, the wall is down and I can see the land's terraced descent. Low hills I couldn't see before roll at the base of the mountains. Now within view, the old logging road winds down the hillside like a country lane.

These are the rewards of tending the land.

spring drama

The weather changes suddenly. Snow piles still hunker at the end of the driveway and next to the house, settling under the warm sun of the spring summer day.

I sit on the back porch, stunned with pleasure. Here is a remarkable moment in the quietude of the country. As the snow moves infinitesimally toward extinction, I hear icy crystals sink into melted spaces, quietly crunching as they move.

A California friend, who has sympathetically followed our snowstormed spring weather news, calls to ask how I'm holding up.

"I am sitting outside in shirtsleeves," I tell him. "Listening to the snow melt."

His sigh crosses the miles from San Diego's endless-summer. "I cannot even imagine," he says.

I rake thatch out of the lawn with a taped hand, nursing a strain from lifting heavy, wet snow over the front porch railing just days before.

The birds, who had fed so furiously between storms, seem to lack faith in the good weather fortune. My flocks of finches, chickadees, nuthatches, jays, and sparrows continue to feed in droves.

A resident hawk lives in my woods. I am affectionately attached to him. When I first looked at this house and land, I was a refugee from a broken life seeking a new home. As I surveyed the backyard from the trailhead at the edge of the woods, the hawk circled high in a summer blue sky, calling.

In the two and a half years since, I have rarely caught glimpses of the hawk but have heard him often. Mourning doves, a favorite hawk prey, have been conspicuously absent from my bird population. Occasionally, one or two will appear for a few days. Their haunting, repetitive coos will just begin to irritate me when silence descends again.

I am washing dishes and watching birds at the feeder. A mourning dove makes a rare appearance, flying in to peck at fallen seeds. Inexplicably, the feathered hordes abandon the feeding site. The dove is alone.

Idly, I think of the hawk.

As the thought flickers in my mind, something blurred and brown plummets from above, beyond my view. The dove disappears. A puff of gray-blue feathers erupts from the shroud of motion. The hawk materializes and flies to roost on a dead branch of a nearby pine.

Somehow, the dove has escaped, leaving only those feathers behind.

The hawk, perhaps stunned by his unsuccessful dive into the ground, rests in clear view on the branch. Grabbing my glasses, I savor the sight. Suddenly, he glides toward me, landing under the feeder. Perhaps confirming the absence of his prey.

Then he lifts himself onto the edge of the deck, mere feet from the window. He turns his head and stares directly at me. His eyes are, chillingly, blood red. We regard each other for long seconds. Then, he swoops away into the woods.

I am happy not to be a mourning dove.

we have liftoff

To fully savor the sweetness of the North Country's brief spring and summer flings, a screened-in refuge is imperative. Especially if you live close to the woods.

Blackflies invade the lovely days of May. Mosquitoes move in for the duration. I accept the foul-smelling repellents necessary for outdoor chores and the ritual of application and subsequent showering off.

But sometimes I just want to be outside. To breathe in the dawn. To sit in the dark and stare at stars, without drenching myself in insecticides.

If you're not blessed with a screen porch, you are consigned to the mercies of backyard tent or gazebo products. On which, unfortunately, I am becoming an expert.

The year before last, Tom bought me a rig we nicknamed The Lunar Landing Module. Hello, Houston. The six-sided dome suited my backyard perfectly. Its rounded structure rested comfortably on the gentle hillock beneath shading pines.

That first year, it didn't go up until the last days of June, and we disassembled it in early September. It was delightful.

Last year, we put it up in mid-May. When we took it down, the fabric ripped. All told, The Lunar Landing Module lasted for five months and change. It wasn't surprising that the company's "one year guarantee" extended from point of purchase, not taking into account months of actual use.

What was surprising was the company's assertion that the product was classified as a "tent," for camping purposes—not intended to be left standing. Never mind that on its website, the "tent" was not classified under camping equipment. It was categorized as a "gazebo" in the lawn and garden section.

A few weeks ago, Tom bought a screen gazebo at a local discount store. Its top slightly resembles a pagoda, perhaps reflecting its made-in-China origin. Once assembled, its structure seemed unstable, and I did not have much faith in the wimpy stakes it relied on for additional support.

Sure enough, big winds blew through, inflated the pagoda roof, lifted the whole structure off the ground, and rolled it across the yard.

I give the manufacturers zero points for design, but ten points for materials. Despite its backyard jaunt, the roof was not punctured, nor was the screening torn. With a bit of expert vise work, Tom straightened strategic metal joints. We successfully reassembled the gazebo and secured it with clothesline guyed to heavy-duty stakes.

Even so, when big winds returned last week, I noticed the roof was again inflating. I watched the gazebo strain toward flight against its earthly bindings.

Tom observed that at the rate we're going, it would be cheaper to build an actual, permanent screened-in gazebo. Given what's been spent thus far, he pointed out, "We've already bought the materials."

We'll see how long this one lasts before launching construction. Meanwhile, she has a name. As we retrieved her from her romp, Tom said, "Well, we've had The Lunar Landing Module . . . now we have the Mars Rover."

night visitor

Here's a tale of things that go crunch in the night and living on the edge of wild woods.

When you live in a place for a long time, creepy sounds become benignly familiar. Old houses creak, settling into themselves with such presence it seems someone has entered your home. The wind slides a porch chair across wood, as if a villain sneaks toward the door.

In the wee small hours, unfamiliar sounds are especially alarming, triggering many adrenaline-rush moments. Until you become accustomed to them—then they are comforting.

After seven months in my new home, I began to develop a trusting ease with thumps, bumps, and squealing branches rubbing against one another.

One night, my peace was disturbed by Teddy-dog's strange behavior. From a sound sleep, he suddenly leapt off the bed and rushed to the kitchen. Then he came back, barking and prancing, until I followed him to the back door, where he sat with poised alertness.

This is a disturbing development at three o'clock in the morning.

I peered out the narrow door window and saw nothing untoward. Grabbing my heavy walking staff in one hand, flashlight in the other, I stepped onto the back porch—feeling like I was in a Grade B horror movie. *Oh, no, don't open that door.*

Nothing.

This went on, intermittently, for a week or so. Then I began hearing peculiar noises from the back porch. Finally, one night when I crept out the door, Teddy slipped past me . . . and flushed a porcupine from under the porch.

Teddy weighs maybe twenty pounds but, being part terrier, he's stubborn and fierce in my defense. I cannot believe he actually obeyed when I yelled *no* and *come*. Really, I'm not sure which came first—he got a quill in his nose and decided coming was a prudent option, or he got only one quill because he turned to obey.

A couple of nights later, I heard what I first thought were mice trying to chew their way into the house . . . but realized they'd have to be the biggest mice in the world to produce *that* gnawing noise. From the kitchen window, I saw the porcupine under the steps, chewing at the wood.

I didn't know porcupines would attack wood with a fervor that would make a beaver proud. I've been assured by state wildlife folks that this is perfectly normal porcupine behavior. (Oh, goodie, my porcupine is normal.) A salt deficiency in their diet makes pressure-treated wood a saline treat.

They also informed me that once porcupines find a salty source, they're unlikely to give it up. Maybe so, but maybe my porcupine is really smart. Since the cage trap was set on his trail at the edge of the woods, he has not returned.

I'm grateful. If he's caught, it's a death sentence.

Stay away, quilled creature.

wild gifts

If I still lived at my former home, I would be battling black-flies and clearing my gardens of winter's detritus. Here at my new home, in this crippled spring of clouds and rain, I'm spending more time observing than doing.

This watchful practice is an enduring gift from the old place. There, I learned that old-timers had reasons for doing things as they did. These lessons were often learned only when I had undone something and realized its wisdom after the fact.

There, I gradually discovered the virtue of waiting. Left alone, weeds invading the garden sometimes blossomed into entrancing wildflowers. Like the old-timers, nature reveals its artistry through cycles and seasons.

On the north side of my driveway, the land rises slightly to the woods. It's studded with exposed ledge and sparse grass. "If you want a decent lawn here," folks observed last fall when I moved in, "you'll have to get some fill."

"Mmm-hmmm," I replied noncommittally. I didn't want to appear ungrateful for their advice, but I was waiting. Before I buried the rocky hillside, I wanted to see what it had to offer.

In spring's early, sunny days, clusters of tiny white flowers appeared amid the thin grass. Up close, each minute petal was shaded with blue. Forget-me-nots. With each day, the clusters multiplied. Behind the garage, they're so thick I walk in wide circles to avoid crushing the delightful blossoms.

Here and there are scattered wild violets, both white and purple. I was also surprised by white, star-shaped flowers with golden centers. They're so close to the ground, I might not have noticed them had I not been treasure hunting.

In my backyard, near the stone-laid fire pit, there is a small but tall young tree I couldn't identify. I pruned some lower branches and otherwise left it alone. This week, it blossomed with clusters of delicate white flowers. It might be some kind of ash. I'm not sure; I'm still learning how to navigate the Internet for arboreal identifications.

Some gifts take longer to reveal themselves. On the southern side of my front yard, prickly, whippy vines cluster along the forest's edge. I was tempted to cut them down so I could easily enter the woods there. But late last fall, their fading leaf patterns looked familiar. Now I'm almost sure they're wild raspberries. Next to them grows a stretch of what might be puckerbrush, but then again, might be blackberries.

I'll wait and see.

Down by the road, I had pruners in hand to take down a scrawny, scraggly thing. Not quite sapling, not quite vine, it looked just awful. But whispered wisdom stayed my hand, and now I know it is wild rose, its potential beauty disguised by dormancy.

Wild gifts are the rewards of waiting.

porcupine pranks

A few weeks ago, I wrote a column featuring a porcupine that was snacking regularly on my back deck.

The wildlife experts informed me that, having found a yummy source of saltiness in the pressure-treated wood, the critter would inevitably return. With all due respect for my heartfelt reluctance to kill the creature, game warden Kevin Carvey said it really was the only option.

What about trapping and relocating it, I asked.

We don't like to move wild animals, he explained. They may have some kind of illness, and if we relocate them, we'd introduce the sickness to a different animal population. There's a twist I hadn't considered. That's me. Typhoid Mary of the porcupine clan.

All you folks out there who own firearms and are experienced hunters are probably saying, "What's the problem?" And, in fact, Kevin initially raised the same question.

"When wildlife is doing property damage, you have the right to kill it," he said.

Then he paused and clarified. "Well, most of the time. I wouldn't tell someone they could kill a bear that was getting into their garbage. I'd tell them to take their garbage inside . . . But I can't very well tell you to take your porch inside, can I?"

I suspect Kevin has a potential second career as a stand-up comedian.

Having established that not only do I not own a firearm, I have no experience with guns, Kevin and I agreed that the vision of me playing shoot-'em-up in my backyard wasn't a pretty sight. Ergo, enter Melvin Nunn of Groton.

Melvin brought me a trap—baiting it with a salt-soaked rag—and set it up where I'd seen the porcupine waddle off into the woods. Once trapped, the porcupine would be transported and dispatched by Melvin's experienced hands. (Since Teddy-dog wanders these premises, a lethal trap was out of the question.)

At last writing, I was hopeful that my porcupine was the exception to the rule—it hadn't returned. Melvin said that if it didn't come back in four or five days, there was a chance it had moved on.

Then, alas, I awoke one night to the familiar sound of gnawing. This time, when I managed to chase the porcupine away, it went into the woods via another route. I relocated the trap and the next day discovered a lovely, large, but very dead rabbit inside. The poor thing must have died of fright.

Great. Now I'm killing bunny rabbits.

This time, I put the trap at the porcupine's favorite snacking spot—just under the stairs. Melvin said that was worth a try. I refreshed the salty bait . . . and, sure enough, the porcupine returned.

Yep, I heard him at his usual wee-small-hours-of-the-morning snack time.

There he was. Revealed in the full beam of my flashlight, gnawing at delectable spots he hadn't been able to reach until now—from his comfortable, convenient perch on top of the trap.

when garbage was garbage

Every once in a while, we slip into nostalgia. Some say that's a sign of advancing age—when the past appears more delicious than the present. But I think treasuring the qualities of an earlier time is a quirk of memory, a sweetness triggered by fond remembrances, not a red flag for waning mental health.

"Remember when . . ." can be a gentle game to play, even when there's a slight sting of loss or implied social barb. Remember when families sat down to dinner together? Remember when kids played outside till dark, not inside in virtual worlds?

Remember when garbage was garbage? This struck me the other day.

I was dutifully sorting recyclables in the garage. Glass (returnables and non-). Junk mail. Cardboard containers. Plastics (#2). It occurred to me that I am more intimate with my garbage than is seemly.

The organizing gurus tell us that a basic principle of simplification is to handle an item as few times as possible. With my trash, I am in direct and repeated violation of this principle.

Consider the cereal box.

In the grocery store, I put it in my basket. If there are no available baggers (oddly often these days), I pack it into a bag. At home, I unpack it and put it on the shelf. Again and again, I take it down and fill my bowl. Once the box is empty, I crush it and put it in the kitchen can for recycling. I later take it to the garage. I pack it with others of its kind. When I make my periodic trip to the recycling center, I finally toss it into the appropriate container.

That's more physical contact than I have with my closest friends.

Don't get me wrong. I believe in taking responsibility for stewardship of my trash. My indoctrination began at an early age, before "recycle" was a common word in the social vocabulary.

When I was a little girl, a Brownie in the Girl Scouts, we were taught to leave a place cleaner than we found it. I picked up after others at campsites. Later in my Scout career, backpacking into the heights of Yosemite, I learned to pack out what I packed in. That included garbage.

Few things inspire as much disgust with my fellow humans as finding my way to some place of natural beauty, only to be greeted by beer cans and Twinkie wrappers.

In my childhood home, trash was trash. It went into the trash can in the kitchen, then into the can that was set by the side of the road, where the garbagemen picked it up.

And that was that.

Ignorance wasn't good for the earth, but in retrospect it was blissful.

So, I do my duty as a domestic waste engineer, but allow me a politically incorrect moment or two of nostalgia for those simple days when trash just got thrown away . . .

. . . back when garbage was garbage.

ticked off

I've had a permanent case of the heebie-jeebies ever since my first close encounter with a tick this summer. I know I'm not alone in this revulsion anxiety.

More folks responded to my June tick column than to any I've written in a long time. In the grocery store, at the bank, on the street, via email, readers have regaled me with stories of their own. Where they got ticks, how they got them, what they did when they got them. How their family, friends, and acquaintances got them.

Apparently, I've become the public therapist for tick trauma.

In view of the service I've provided, it's only fair that I get to columnize my own experiences with tick mania.

Late one afternoon, while on the phone with my friend Dee in Maine, I idly ran my fingers through my hair. Just above my hairline on the back of my neck, I encountered a crusty hardness. Tick fear and hysteria took over.

Coached long-distance by Dee, I dashed to the bathroom, grabbed a hand mirror, and began contorting myself in front of the large mirror. Given my dark brown hair, the black scabby place, and the fact that I am not an owl, I couldn't determine if I'd gotten a nasty bug bite or if a tick had taken residence in my flesh.

Dee's vision being of no help, I hung up, grabbed a large magnifying glass, and got into my car. Determined to accost the first pair of eyes I encountered, I headed into Ryegate Corner . . . which was uncharacteristically crowded with cars.

I'd forgotten this was the church's Strawberry Buffet day.

In the slow traffic, I recognized my neighbor Gail Brown's van coming the other way. As she drew alongside, I frantically asked her to pull over. Confused but responding to my urgency, she did, and launched from her van with apron flapping.

It is a measure of our collective disgust with ticks that Gail was instantly sympathetic and sprang into action. There, on the side of the road, with nicely dressed folks headed for the church supper looking on curiously, Gail pawed through my hair and peered through the magnifying glass.

She dug an old napkin out of her car, we wet it with tea (with lemon and honey) from my travel mug, and she cleaned the wound to be absolutely sure there was no embedded tick.

There was not. With empathetic emphasis, Gail brushed aside my apology for waylaying her and continued on her catsup quest for supper patrons.

The kicker to this tale is that, when I got into town for my grocery shopping, my fingers found another scabby place on top of my head.

One of the friendly clerks sympathetically checked me out in the parking lot.

In the end, this isn't really a tick horror tale. It's a celebration of small-town life, of shared stresses and warmhearted willingness to help.

wild wildflowers

When I moved to my new home, I decided I did not want to re-create the formal gardens I had at the old place.

Let me define "formal garden." I'm no expert, and I did not have elaborate flower beds by Martha Stewart standards. But I did have three long stretches delineated from the grass, planted with perennials strategically positioned for best effect. That was "formal" to me.

Over the years I cultivated those gardens, it was a perpetual battle to keep the grass from sneaking in and taking over. No matter what kind of mulch I used, I was pressed into constant clashes with weeds. On one garden battlefront, the forest repeatedly attacked from the rear.

My new place is surrounded by woods. Given my experience, it was a no-brainer to see that establishing any formal garden would pit me against the superior forces of nature. The better part of valor was, clearly, to choose a different strategy.

My neighbor Darryl came by with a rototiller, perfect for my new plan. I would put in wildflower gardens.

Of the four wildflower gardens I planted, only one took. The others suffered from poor placement choices—flooded out, overtaken by ferns, conquered by grass. I surrendered with equanimity . . . or so I thought.

This spring, the sole surviving wildflower garden was peppered with grass. Between rains, I began the delicate operation of ripping out the interlopers without uprooting the emerging flowers.

I was absolutely, possessively manic to reclaim this garden. To create order within the boundaries I had established. I won't admit to just how long it took me to realize I was doing precisely what I had determined I would not do.

Suffice it to say, the light did dawn. I sat back on my heels. I gathered my tools. I put them away. I surrendered.

At the library one evening, I shared this tale with two women who also love flowers.

"I think the whole idea of wildflower *gardens* is an illusion," Peggy said. "Wildflowers grow in meadows. They grow wild . . ."

I stopped cutting the ragged borders of my yard at the edges of the woods. Wildflowers have proliferated among the grasses and weeds. I stopped mowing the ledge-riddled plot beside my garage. It has become a wildflower meadow.

I am surrounded by daisies and lavender straw asters, by bright yellow and orange blossoms whose names I do not know. Delicate miniature buttercups glow under storm-dark skies. Red clover grows tall and flowers with such vibrancy I am astonished.

Wild roses peek through grassy veils, shockingly pink. Not one was planted by me.

They grew wild, when I let them.

turn it off

Every once in a while, my computer malfunctions in wildly erratic ways. It spits incomprehensible error messages at me. And it won't respond to standard methods of clearing its electronic neural pathways.

This happens when I've been multi-tasking for a prolonged period. Researching on the Internet, I'll bounce among websites in pursuit of some juicy fact. Racing along the information highway, flipping back to my notes to cut 'n' paste gems of data.

Then everything freezes up, and those screaming error messages erupt.

When I seek advice, the wizards of the wired world lead me through a labyrinth of problem-solving procedures. Usually none work—until they come to their last resort.

"Turn the machine off," they say with resignation, clearly disappointed that their complex, elegant solutions have failed.

"Turn the machine *off*?"

Inevitably, this fiasco always unfolds when I'm on deadline. I'm caught in the whirlwind of facts and ideas. Edgy with panic that something's seriously wrong with the equipment I depend on. Shutting down is an outrageous concept.

"Turn it off." I feel the shrug of shoulders from some distant tech center. "Let it rest a few minutes. Then turn it back on. We don't know why it works, but it usually does."

Gritting my teeth, I do as I'm told . . . and when we reengage, the computer is calmly compliant.

You would think I could retain this simple solution. You'd think the wired wizards would offer it up first, not last, in their litany of procedures. I don't. They don't.

Why not?

Stop. Rest. Clear the decks. Even electronic devices get overloaded. This is hardly rocket science.

Recently, when this scenario played itself out for the umpteenth time, I didn't rush to turn the computer back on. An absurdly obvious idea came to me—what's good for computers is good for people, too.

Turn it off.

Do you know anyone who actually takes a lunch break anymore? Versus those who "do meetings" at lunch, or eat at their desks?

There's a zillion-dollar relaxation industry—books and instructional CDs, tapes, workshops—geared to teach us how to unwind. How to stop. Is this not bizarre? Relaxation has become a lost art that now requires study.

And I wonder, is it possible to relax while one *studies* relaxation?

Here in the North Country, we're surrounded by natural beauty. We could ask for no better blessing to quiet the noise in our minds. But how many of us hear the error messages screeching from our bodies and spirits and stop to take a wandering walk in the woods? Or watch a hawk circling overhead?

I was past deadline as I wrote this column. I could not come up with a strong closing. I surrendered and went out on my back deck to sit. Quietly contemplating the woods, I discerned a slight movement between branches and brush. A graceful doe emerged, leading her two fawns.

They are the first deer I've seen since moving to my new home.

the loss of a friend

A dear friend died in May. I haven't been able to write about Penny until now, so keenly have I felt her loss.

She would hate it if I wrote about her in maudlin tones. To honor her, to reflect on how our friendship enriched my life, I had to wait until I was beyond the initial stages of grieving.

Penny played a major role in the development of "Rambling Reflections." She was a merciless critic, expert but always supportive—especially in the beginning when I wasn't sure if I was a writer at all. The style I have developed was tempered in the heat of Penny's uncompromising passion for excellence.

Penny loved the *Journal Opinion*. Born and raised in Salinas, California—in her day, a rural agricultural area—she felt an affinity with North Country life as reflected in these pages. She left Salinas in the early 1940s and lived in a metropolitan area from then on, but reading the *JO* kindled in Penny a special delight.

She said the articles, pictures, and Town News columns depicted a way of life she recognized but had lost touch with. Penny was a woman of decidedly strong opinions. Acerbically critical of many elements of contemporary American lifestyles, she celebrated the enduring down-home values she saw in accounts of the North Country.

Penny was one of my mother's closest friends for nearly thirty years—from the time I was about twelve until my mother's death, the day before my forty-first birthday. I will read-ily admit that when I was a kid, Penny Evans intimidated the heck out of me.

She was not a warm and fuzzy lady. She had the no-non-sense, uncompromising regal air of an older Katharine Hep-burn. Intimidated me? Penny flat-out scared me.

My friendship with Penny began days after my mother's death. I was doing battle with the dragon ladies of the wom-en's club Mom had helped to found. They were giving me a hard time about the memorial service I was arranging in their space. Intuitively I knew I needed a dragon-slayer—and there was none better than Penny.

I was right. She gave me excellent advice. Mom's service was held in the place dear to her, and doors opened between Penny and myself. She became my first, close woman friend of an older generation.

I sing the praises of such friendships. They are rich and too rare.

Penny and I were on opposite sides of the generation gap in the tumultuous '60s. Our conversations on that topic were always heated. She remained convinced that my generation had done its damnedest to destroy the country. We never agreed on any political or social topic, past or present. But invariably, her sharp reasoning demanded that I acknowledge a point of view radically different from my own.

Penny once told me that if she had her professional life to live over again, she'd be an editor. I wish her reincarnation could be accelerated.

I miss Penny.

wildlife encounters, continued

For those who missed the earlier installment, let's recap the porcupine adventures.

There is something salty in the pressure-treated wood of my deck that quilled creatures crave. Especially after a good rain, they crawl out of the dark woods in the wee small hours and gnaw to their heart's content.

They are particularly fond of the steps.

I say "they" because, though I once thought there was only one, it turns out there are two porcupines. Having chased both of them, I know. One is slim and fast; the other is fat and slow.

Why am I chasing porcupines? Because I have no expertise with guns, and attempts to trap them have failed. Regular readers will recall that the trapping endeavor was terminated when I spotted a porcupine standing on top of the trap, reaching for a particularly tasty section of the deck.

I've been reduced to the most primitive means of battle. I am a night person, so I'm awake in the stillness of the small hours when gnawing noises are hard to miss. I've been keeping a stout walking stick by my back door.

Upon hearing feasting sounds, I would grab it, go outside and beat the sides of deck. This would bring the porcupine out from his late-night snacking under the porch, and I'd whack the creature as many times as possible before it retreated into the woods.

The theory was, sooner or later they'd tire of this abuse and leave my deck alone.

Porcupines are either masochists or very, very stubborn.

One night recently, I heard the chomping and flew into a temper. I'd had a bad day. I'd had it with the porcupine dance. In an angry rush, I slipped on some shoes but did not fasten them.

You know that little voice you sometimes hear that whispers, "Bad idea!" and other wise counsel? That voice of intuition, clairvoyance, or divine guidance? The little voice that—when ignored—generally proves to be right? Well, that voice said, "If you don't get these shoes on your feet properly, you're going to trip."

In my fury, I ignored this counsel, snatched my stick and banged the side of the deck. When the porcupine popped his head out between the stairs, I turned to attack it. That's when my shoes and my feet parted company.

My little toe got caught in the space between the deck boards. My body kept moving forward, my toe stayed where it was, and I went down.

As I lay on the deck with the unmistakable pain of a broken bone shooting from my toe, the porcupine danced away.

I was fortunate that ignoring that small voice didn't extract a greater toll. I could have taken a header down the stairs.

The next porcupine strategy comes from a friend of Native American ancestry. He says throwing a heavy blanket over the creature will cause it to release its quills. Since porcupines don't like to run around without a full defense system, they'll be discouraged from returning.

Stay tuned.

I never did toss a blanket and, eventually, the porcupines simply stopped showing up.

autumn slide

Autumn approaches like a shy maiden.

She stands at the edge of the dance floor, swaying to the music, tapping her foot in a rhythm all her own.

She does not join the dancers, but slips out to the patio where she weaves moonbeams and shadows in a solitary waltz.

Though days are often summer-like, autumn glides in with dawn and sashays into the evening. The air is tender, cool—as if gently preparing us for the winter ahead. I sit on my back porch, cozy-wrapped in a small blanket brought from my bed, watching dawn flame through the trees.

Summer throws her final fling. My wildflower garden is dominated by black-eyed Susans. Rich buttery gold, staring dark centers. Few of the more delicate early flowers remain . . . nature knows heartier stock is best for these transition days.

Late one afternoon, Tom and I return to my place after running errands. We are astonished at the sight of dozens of dragonflies soaring, dodging, rising, dipping above the yard at the edge of the woods. The swarm swirls in intricate flight patterns, the envy of any air traffic controller.

Entranced, we approach tentatively, not wanting to disperse them. The dragonflies are oblivious, undisturbed as we move closer . . . and closer.

In hushed voices, we wonder. Is this a mating ritual? What draws them together in this aerial display?

We sneak up the stairs onto the porch. Their interlacing acrobatics flow on. The circle of dragonfly flight—rising, dipping, with lightning-fast turns to avoid collision—is hypnotic. The sensation is similar to standing at the ocean's edge, lulled by the rhythmic ebb and flow of waves sliding up the sand.

Tom leaves the porch, walks slowly into the swarm, and sits beneath their center on the grass. I stay where I am, quietly amazed at the sight of him surrounded, as if by fairies flitting on gossamer wings.

While I'm spellbound, Tom closely observes the dragonflies.

"They're feeding!" he says, with the exaltation of discovery.

Sure enough, there are small bugs rising from the grass and from the brush at woods' edge. The dragonflies dodge one another to make quick snatches at them, then—successful or not—circle up, down, around again.

Then Tom notices that some dragonflies spit out parts of the bugs they've eaten. We could see the rejected bits falling. We laugh. Are these dragonflies finicky eaters, consuming only the tastiest parts?

On the porch, I am buzzed by dragonflies so near that I can hear the chattering of their wings.

The chattering of dragonfly wings. Have you ever heard it?

Then one alights next to me. Its large body bears markings like the turquoise stones of Native American jewelry. I barely have time to marvel at its beauty before the dragonfly is off again, joining the dance in flight.

What a gift at summer's end, as autumn slides in.

afterword

Writing a weekly newspaper column often feels like rolling up a message, slipping it into a bottle, and tossing it out to the community. It's not unusual (especially when the writing comes hard) to wonder if anyone is reading me at all.

Months go by, and then it happens. A note comes in the mail or shows up in my inbox. Lovely words from readers who have been touched or entertained by something I've written. Sometimes, their words are more poetic and moving than the column they're responding to. It is genuinely humbling.

I have received letters from people who lived in the North Country for nearly a lifetime, then moved to warmer climates. These folks subscribe to the *Journal Opinion* to stay connected to a place they still love. The simple details of my column awaken memories of the land and communities that brought them joy, and they share those joyful memories with me.

My column is conversational in tone and often personal in content. Readers respond in an equally personal way.

They tell me they've been comforted by my expressions of grief and loss and share their own stories. When I write about the sustaining strength bestowed by the natural beauties of the North Country, they tell me they find strength. There are few things more rewarding to a writer than knowing her words have eased someone else's pain.

The small towns of the *Journal Opinion* community weave an intertwining web. We patronize a limited number of shops, congregate in a few general stores, do our banking at a handful of banks, eat at the same diners, visit local libraries, attend neighborhood churches, and go to post offices where the postmaster is likely to be a neighbor.

In such an intimate world, a columnist for the local paper becomes a very public figure.

Many people I've never met know who I am. I cannot count the times a stranger has overheard my name and turned to say, "You're Nessa Flax? I read your article all the time . . ." And the conversation begins.

What I love about these encounters is that the column inspires an unusual intimacy in casual conversations. Readers tell me their stories, their feelings, their opinions and beliefs, transforming mundane errand runs into enriching experiences.

Five hundred publishable words a week, for sixteen years and counting. It would not have been possible, it would not be possible, without the notes in the mail—electronic or snail—without the encounters on the street, in the bank and grocery store, at the diner and post office . . . without my bottled messages washing back onto my shores.

acknowledgments

Some writers thrive on the solitude that comes with the craft; I am not one of them.

So, first and foremost, immeasurable gratitude to Cicely Richardson, without whom this book would not exist. Alone, I would not have survived the journey through some twelve years of columns to this final destination. And heaven knows I could not have paid for the years of collaboration we shared, nor would I have found an editor who could read my intent with the familiarity we forged over a decade at the *Journal Opinion.*

Thanks also to my first editor at the newspaper, Charlie Glazer. He always says he did little for me. Don't believe him.

Although most of these columns predate my working relationship with current *JO* editor Alex Nuti-de Biasi, his influence is not absent. Editing the old with Cicely, it was impossible not to see through the lens of working with Alex in the present.

A posthumous debt of gratitude is owed to Penny Evans of Oakland, California. She believed in me as a writer long before I did. Penny said she wanted to be an editor in her next life: I hope she reincarnates while I'm still writing.

Heartfelt hugs to Tom Bryer, man of all trades, who eased the transition from the old home to the new in more ways than can be described here.

Preparing the original submission packet for Bunker Hill Publishing, I called on a diverse group of reader-friends to help me choose the five ("*only* five!") columns to represent the manuscript. Clearly, their input was invaluable. Thank you to Mike Mickleson, who appreciates the columns from Hamilton, Montana; ninety-plus-year-old native Vermonter Alice McLure; retired Ryegate farmers Holly and Nick McLure; local artist Marie Witte; and good neighbors Ron Cressy and Kevin Proctor.

Kevin also has my special gratitude for patiently stalking the foliage during a particularly pesky fall to get a good shot for the book cover.

For their interest in this project and for holding my body, mind, and spirit together during the long labor of *Voices'* birth, I'm grateful to acupuncturist Amy Wheeler and chiropractor Dr. Marc Sinclair.

A warm embrace to former student and fencer Heather McClintock, whose willingness to contribute her considerable professional skills for a simple author photo added another ring to the circle of friends bringing this book into being.

Thank you to Dick McCormack, who allowed me to borrow his song title, and for writing lyrics that model the best of storytelling.

What-would-I-do-without-you appreciation to longtime friend Nils Rosenquest of San Francisco, who guided me through my first book contract, and to Dee Drugach of Nobleboro, Maine, who answered my all-hours calls for reader feedback and general hand-holding.

To Ib and Carole Bellew of Bunker Hill Publishing, my gratitude for your dedication to values rare in today's book business . . . and for helping make my dream come true.

My experience with copy editor Laura Jorstad took the terror out of a potentially traumatic stage of publishing. With wit, intelligence, and an overarching respect for the writer's voice, *acknowledgments*

Laura helped me polish the book to its final sheen. And in the process, I found a kindred spirit of words and woods.

Many people appear in the columns throughout this collection. To all of you, many thanks for enriching my life and for allowing me to steal your best lines.